KILLING THE COVER LETTER

How to Get a Job in Advertising & Public Relations in a Changed World

Gene Kincaid

Published in the United States by Hale Fred Press, Austin, Texas.
Printed by Lulu Enterprises, Inc., Morrisville, NC.

ISBN-13: 978-0-615-25540-8

PRINTED IN THE UNITED STATES OF AMERICA

Contents

Acknowledgements

Without help from five people, this book would not exist.

Laura Kincaid, my daughter, provided the initial coverage.
A talented film editor, Laura's command of storytelling logic and
her sense of narrative structure brought purpose and order to a
chaotic draft.

Maria Rivera, fellow faculty member in the Department of
Advertising at UT-Austin and freelance copywriter/owner of
The Little Red Writing Shop in Austin, was the book's development editor. With a deft hand, Maria lifted the book's voice to its
intended level — honest, upbeat encouragement. She also found
the perfect book title amid a pile of words and spoken thoughts.

Paula Minahan, freelance copywriter and longtime friend, was the
book's copy editor. Paula's discipline swiftly tightened every paragraph and every page, much to the book's benefit. Quite simply,
her meticulous care brought the book into the mainstream by
removing my writing idiosyncrasies.

David Horridge, freelance creative director and former colleague
in the Department of Advertising at UT-Austin, designed the
book. David's graphic eye relaxed everything. He gently pushed
aside intimidating blocks of text and cleared the reader's work
surface, allowing you to get down to the important business of
finding a job. I can hardly believe I wrote the printed words, they
don't reflect the hammer blows I delivered to my keyboard.

Kim Swift created the illustrations and cover art. Without this
original artwork, you, the reader, never would have opened the
book or reached this page. Graphics trump text. Interesting.

Finally, I must acknowledge the deep debt of gratitude I owe to all of my students. A handful will read their first names in the book, laugh out loud, then e-mail me to administer some well-deserved ribbing. It will be a treat to hear from you. Other students will read the book and e-mail criticisms, suggestions, corrections and encouragement. Turnabout is fair play. It will be a treat to hear from you, too.

Introduction

Ten years after the birth of the Internet, the advertising and public relations industries are in the midst of a sea change. The Internet fundamentally altered the global communications landscape and continues to change our world daily.

The fact that you might have jumped onto the Internet and visited webster.com or wikipedia.org to look up the definition of "sea change" is ample evidence of the rapid, disruptive and transforming changes taking place in both advertising and public relations.

That you effortlessly understand "webster.com" to be a contraction of "http://www.webster.com" reinforces this fact.

The reality that you unquestioningly accept the very notion of an online encyclopedia where anyone, anywhere, at any time, can change any entry is utterly astonishing. That wikipedia.org is rapidly adapting and changing this novel editorial practice to address mischievous behavior speaks to the ever-evolving nature of our new technologies.

Today's digital panorama is filled with earbuds, ring tones, podcasts, IM, social networking web sites, fully Internet-enabled cell phones and consumer desktop computers with processing power once reserved for mainframes. We are approaching communications capacity — the ability to touch anyone, anywhere, at any time.

In this changed world, we're moving away from the era of "mass communications" that began with Gutenberg's printing press, to a world of "negotiated communications," wherein an advertiser must earn their way into a consumer's limited communications patterns. In that world, the advertising and public relations industries will operate under a completely different set of assumptions and rules than those practiced for the past 60 years. The new rules will rest on a single fact: The audience is in control.

This applies to job hunting. Today's young public relations and advertising professionals are required to earn their way into commercial conversations. Job hunters must identify a tightly defined audience, then find interesting ways to initially capture a key audience member's attention. They must deliver highly relevant and practical messages during an interview, use the right kind of frequency after the interview to maintain momentum, and then create new opportunities to "ask for the job."

This is the sea change.

The half-century-old principles of mass communications used for job hunting no longer hold: Create a resumé. Mail it to dozens of agencies. Fill out a profile on a job-hunting web site where "thousands of employers" will see it.

"What? No more cover letters?!" Gasp.

You're about to do some hard work that gives you a very powerful substitute.

Killing the Cover Letter – How to Get a Job in Advertising & Public Relations in a Changed World is based on my experiences as a Senior Lecturer in the Department of Advertising at the University of Texas at Austin. It began as a collection of bits of advice repeated again and again over 15 years to successive waves of very bright students, who passed (some might say "suffered") through my classes in Integrated Communications Management, Advertising & PR Campaigns, One-to-One Advertising on the Internet, and Digital Media.

This book reflects my assessment of the changes taking place within advertising and public relations. It also reaches back into the pre-Internet world and drags forward timeless business tactics that will weather the current revolution.

Finally, this book embodies my deeply felt belief regarding teaching: My job is to help students succeed. I've learned the best way to accomplish this is by putting challenging problems in front of very smart students, then getting out of their way. This book puts an action plan within your grasp. Expect success.

Gene Kincaid
Austin, Texas
Fall 2008

PART I
Why This Book?

1. Anyone Can Do This, but Everyone Won't

On October 4, 2000, I wrangled a breakfast with Mr. Keith Reinhard, Chairman of DDB Worldwide, and Ms. Pat Sloan, Sr. VP Corporate Director of Public Affairs for DDB Worldwide, prior to their formal speaking engagements at a University of Texas distinguished speaker series. The stated purpose of the breakfast was to introduce both individuals to six of my interactive advertising students. The real purpose was to demonstrate the untapped opportunities offered to those who understand that everyone eats breakfast, including visiting chairmen and corporate directors.

As you might expect, Keith and Pat were wonderfully adept at responding to questions from, and then comfortably directing questions to, the six students. Once the students figured out that both of our guests were genuinely interested in hearing what they had to say about interactive advertising, the breakfast meeting turned into a very lively conversation. One of the students then drove Keith and Pat to campus with plenty of time to spare before their first appointment of the day.

In April 2002, one of the six students, Cody, was planning a job-hunting trip to New York and asked me if I had any advice. She was shocked when, after reminding her of our breakfast meeting with Mr. Reinhard, I suggested she set up a meeting with him while in New York.

"I can't just call the Chairman of DDB Worldwide and request a meeting."

"Why not? You had an hour-long breakfast meeting with him, didn't you?"

"Yes."

"He seemed pretty interested in what you had to say about interactive advertising, didn't he?"

"Yes."

"And Tribal DDB is a big interactive player, aren't they?"

"Yes."

"Well, give Keith a call. You'll probably work through his executive assistant, so let her know you had breakfast with Mr. Reinhard in Austin. See if he's available for a 15-minute meeting. The worse thing that can happen is that Keith isn't in town that day, or his schedule won't allow time for a visit. I'd make the call if I were in your boots."

Cody made the call and set up the meeting. She also did her homework on DDB before leaving and, because she was interested in global communications, she read up on Dentsu, the world's largest advertising agency. Her 15-minute meeting turned into a 45-minute meeting once Keith learned that Cody was current on the goings on at Dentsu. It turns out he was leaving for Japan the

RECRUITERS AND ON-CAMPUS VISITS

AIRPORT PICK-UP Call the interviewer's office three to four days before they're scheduled to leave and ask for the airline's arriving flight number and time. Get a URL with a photo of the person on the agency's web site. Meet the recruiter and take them to their hotel.

 This demonstrates the ability to be proactive and assertive, gives you 20 minutes of uninterrupted time with the recruiter, communicates they're important, and indicates you know how to treat arriving clients.

BREAKFAST Everybody eats breakfast. Call ahead and offer to meet for breakfast on their first day, and drive the person to campus with plenty of time to spare for their first meeting. Arrive early, select a table, tell the waiter you're on a tight schedule, and immediately tip $5. When the recruiter arrives, catch their attention and tell them the waiter knows you're both on a schedule. Order, chat, pay when served, then eat — this is business, you're the timekeeper, move things along. You're driving the conversation and the car, so it's OK to look at your watch.

 This indicates you understand business travel, the necessity to start early, stay on an agenda and enforce a schedule. It also displays your ability to diplomatically move conversations along — a handy client skill to have.

AIRPORT DROP-OFF Return trips to the airport come late in the day when everyone is tired. Call the recruiter's office three to four days *before* they come to campus. Ask for the airline's departure flight number and time, and offer to pick the recruiter up after their last appointment to take them to the airport.

 This gives you a few minutes with the recruiter and demonstrates pre-planning organizational skills — critical points in the business process. It also means you're the last candidate they see before returning home, affirms they're important and demonstrates you already know how to manage client relations from start to finish.

next day and wanted a quick update on what Cody had read. That led to a personal introduction by Keith to the head of interactive advertising at DDB, which is not a bad way to start a job hunt at a major agency.

The approach described in this book pushes you to identify the most important decision-maker to you, earn your way into an initial conversation with this person, and then use relevant, frequent contact to maintain a presence in their mind.

In a Nutshell

If you cringe at the idea of writing hundreds of cover letters and mailing out hundreds of resumés in hopes of finding a job, this book is for you.

If you constantly avoid phone calls from your parents because they want you to move back home and look for a job in your hometown, this book is for you.

If you're feeling overwhelmed and lost because you know you need to start looking for a job but don't know exactly how, where or when to start, this book is for you.

If you're beginning to think no one cares about you, no one has time for you, no one will return your phone call — much less help you get started — this book is for you.

Here's why. This little book turns the job-hunting process on its ear by adopting a new, somewhat radical point of view. In a few pages, it proposes that you forget everything you were ever told about how to look for a job. It asks that you increase your workload just prior to graduation. And it asks you to accept a job-hunting process that doesn't focus on you at a time when you're legitimately concerned about yourself and the immediate future.

This book requires you to turn the tables on the job-hunting process and approach it in a fundamentally new way. You must:

• Understand yourself from two distinctly new perspectives we'll discuss in Chapter 5.
• Focus your attention on a handful of agencies and firms.
• Conduct "applied" background research on those companies.
• Quit playing the job-hunting game everyone else is playing.
• Conserve your energy, creativity, motivation and time.
• Start practicing your profession now — before you get hired.

1. **COME IN EARLY, LEAVE LATE.**
Why: You'll get a workhorse reputation.

- Be creative. Think strategically. Innovate as you solve problems.
- Demonstrate the professional characteristics interviewers seek.
- Be willing to do much more than what you think it's going to take to get there.
- Continue doing most of the things outlined in this book — even after you've landed the job.

MULTI-TASKING You're already an expert. Somehow you've mastered the art of studying an open book, talking on the phone, working on your laptop, and taking handwritten notes while plugged into an iPod with the TV and your stereo blasting in the background.

Now do it during your job hunt. But change the type of "tasking."

Welcome Aboard

This book suggests you start your career in advertising and public relations when you start hunting for your first job — right now. You can read this entire book in about three hours, leaving you plenty of time to get started.

Welcome to advertising and public relations.

Come on in. There's plenty of room for you.

You're about to use a job-hunting method that runs counter to what your roommate, classmates and others in a similar situation are doing. You'll be going against advice you've heard (and will hear) from people you know and trust. You will ignore the advice of every college career counseling center. Still listening? You will completely bypass the process your parents tell you to follow. You will get started right now, not "closer to graduation."

Contrary to What You've Heard...

• Don't start with HR

You'll notice there is a distinct absence of Human Resources (HR) in this book. It's not that the HR function isn't important. Not at all. HR plays a valuable role in every business. After all, advertising and public relations agencies are little more than collections of highly motivated and skilled individuals organized into a service business. Humans are obviously at the center of that equation.

It's just that no one gets a job by starting with HR. By law, HR is required to develop and follow processes that treat everyone in an equal, impartial and dispassionate manner. Which is exactly the opposite of how the advertising and public relations agency business works. Advertising and public relations professionals don't treat every member of an audience equally, because that makes no sense from a communications or business standpoint.

Most importantly, HR doesn't truly understand the intricacies, subtleties and refinements of the position you're applying for. HR can't make the razor-thin distinctions and the fine-grain determinations that separate job candidates. HR can't let passion, drive, intensity and the burning desire to pay your dues enter into the equation.

Only the person charged with making the hiring decision can do that. That person is your audience, not HR.

So don't believe starting with HR will get you the job. It won't.

• Don't use online job sites for anything other than low-effort trolling and job-description harvesting.

A software-mediated job search is as cold as it sounds. Use this method only if your resumé is packed with a string of sought-after acronyms: .NET®, Flash®, XSLT®, PHP®, Oracle® and ASP®. Or DART®, IMS®, SRDS®, Qualitap®, @Plan®, MediaMetrix® and AdRelevance®. It will probably work. But if your resumé contains a skill string like those just listed, you might not need this book.

Seven Digital Do's

1. Your e-mail address.

It's possible you created your e-mail address prefix (what appears before the "@" symbol) quite some time ago. Your intent was to stand out in a crowd or make a statement.

As you begin job hunting, however, an overly colorful or evocative e-mail address stands out like a sore thumb on your resumé and business card.

If your current e-mail address is something like "popatop@state-college.edu" or "partygirl18@bigemailcompany.com," consider creating a new e-mail address for your job hunt.

Be distinctive. Be alive. But be a professional. An address like "10toesup10toesdown@wheeee.net" might hurt your credibility and lessen your chances of being considered for the job.

2. The front page of *The Dallas Morning News.*

"Be careful of what you say. It might wind up on the front page of *The Dallas Morning News.*" That advice has circulated for decades within the Texas business community.

Today, things are different. It's easier. It's faster. It's still true.

Copy. Paste. Send.

That's all it takes (and about how long it takes) to forward your words to someone with whom you didn't intend to communicate.

Be aware of this as you rant, flame and dis in the digital world. Your words might wind up on the front page of *The Dallas*

2. **BE 10 MINUTES EARLY TO MEETINGS.**
Why: Allows you to sit next to, or opposite, The Lion.

Morning News. Or worse – because you'll never even know it happened – your words might land in the in-box of a decision-maker you want to interview with.

3. Employers use Facebook.com and MySpace.com, too, but not in the way you use them.

...a party picture of someone twirling on a coffee table with nine empty bottles of rum in the foreground ...someone chugging a beer with a T-shirt pulled up to their chin. These are the images of a group of marketing students found in only 11 minutes of browsing on Facebook.com.

If that's the first visual impression you create in your social networking profile, it may be your last impression.

What you'll hear:
> "Your skills and talents don't match our current requirements. We will retain your resumé for future consideration. Good luck in your job search."

What they're actually saying:
> "Mr. Party Dog needs to grow up. Easy reject. Who's next?"

4. Leave the "To" field blank until you're ready to hit "Send."

Because halfway through your second paragraph, just as you copy and paste a sentence with someone else's name in it, right as you see the word "your" in a line of text instead of the correct word "you're," you mistakenly, prematurely and stupidly hit the "Send" button. Flying fingers do that sometimes.

Leave the "To" field blank as you compose e-mail. Proofread your work. Insert the recipient's e-mail address into the "To" field just prior to hitting "Send."

5. "Date Prefix" your files with "yymmdd."

For example, add "060704" to the beginning of a document's file name you created (or modified) on July 4, 2006, as in "060704SevenThings.doc."

This does two things. First, your files will appear in date order within folders on your computer. You immediately can pick out the most current version, because "060702SevenThings.doc" will be listed above "060707SevenThings.doc."

Second, when you forget the name of a file, simply nibble your way backward through time to find it. Enter today's "yymmdd" into your computer's "Find File" dialog box to see a list of files created today. Enter yesterday's date and hit "Find." Enter the day before yesterday's date and hit "Find."

"When did I send her a follow-up letter?"

Nibble your way back through time to find out.

6. Stay in touch.

This smart point may fade with the explosion of social networking web sites. But then again, it may not.

It's smart to stay in touch with people on a professional level.

If you're like most people, you have at least three e-mail addresses: A free, web-based e-mail address you've used forever, a school-related e-mail address and a junk address for registering on sites that require you to furnish an e-mail address. You also may have accumulated a few addresses from internships, summer employment and temporary jobs. Plus, you are about to pick up your first professional e-mail address as you land your first job.

In this moving-target e-mail landscape, it's imperative you stay in touch. Who knows what e-mail address people have for you? You may have sent everyone a "change-of-address" e-mail — or not. Because your "change-of-address" e-mail had 43 recipients, a spam filter may have snared it — or not. The recipient may have opened it — or not.

If you haven't heard from someone in a long time, you've probably bounced out of their address book. E-mail sent to you starts bouncing. After a while, the sender gets tired of receiving bounced messages from your e-mail provider and they delete your address. Boom, you're out of touch.

It's now your job to stay in touch with people on a professional level.

7. Consider registering the .com domain name containing your name.

As in "genekincaid.com."

3. **DRESS CONSERVATIVELY FOR THE OFFICE.**
Why: Be ready for surprise client or prospect visits.

This is not mission critical. Paying an annual registration fee simply precludes anyone else from using a particular domain name on the Internet.

The entire process will cost you somewhere between $12 and $35 per year to "park" (reserve) a domain name, if the domain name is available. Currently, you can stretch out the length of a registration for up to 100 years, which lowers the annual rate to about $9.99, but you must pay the entire $999 up front. The Trust Department of your bank will love this.

There are many domain registrars. "BetterWhois.com" is a popular site to determine if your .com domain name is available. Visit http://www.betterwhois.com/.

If your .com domain name is available, I suggest you visit http://www.networksolutions.com. With your credit card firmly in hand, set up an account, pay them $34.99 for a one-year registration and see how it feels. Their account manager interface is well organized and it's just a smart thing to do, making you stand out as a professional among rookies.

One Size Does Not Fit All

The methods proposed in this book might not fit you. This book is founded on the belief that creative thinking and problem solving are more important than your recently departed GPA. Your Plan will include a disciplined, self-aware, self-motivated process coupled with incredible persistence.

Although it's not an all-or-none deal, you do have to push past some thresholds to make Your Plan work. But isn't that what advertising and public relations professionals do?

The Process

What you're about to encounter is a surprisingly simple, step-by-step plan that requires discipline and time to execute well. Don't be fooled by its brevity.

It differs from other methods in two respects:

1. It starts from the perspective of the person who may hire you, and not from the about-to-graduate, somewhat disoriented perspective you now hold.

2. It requires you to focus your efforts and then apply those efforts in several new ways.

The Skeleton

Stripped bare of all flesh, the process boils down to the following steps:

• Put yourself through intense inspection, including a view from an industry veteran.
  – Conduct an honest and illuminating self-assessment.
  – Identify your weaknesses from the interviewer's perspective.
  – Get help in rewording your best and worst professional traits.

• Focus your attention.
  – Study hundreds of job descriptions to identify essential job requirements.
  – Narrow your job search to three or four firms in one or two cities.
  – Create a modular, flexible resumé.

• Do the work.
  – Do a significant amount of industry background research.
  – Use your research results to dramatically expand your job-search scope.
  – View competing agencies, the media and clients as job opportunities.

• Patiently build a network, then use the right kind of frequency within that network.
   – Build your network one person at a time.
   – Use frequent, informative follow-up to become known and remembered.

Keep Your Eyes Wide Open

Keep your vision wide; remain open to new possibilities, new combinations and new ideas. The sum of your academic experience prepares you to contribute to the world in new, exciting and perhaps unexpected ways.

But you must see the opportunities. You can't do that with blinders on or your eyes closed.

As you browse the Internet and encounter sites that intrigue or interest you, see if the site has a "Jobs," "Careers" or "Positions Open" link. If so, and there's a position that fits you, fire off an e-mail inquiry. The invitation exists. Take advantage of it.

During the off-season, well before graduation when the market is flooded with job hunters, conduct a few micro-burst interviews with top executives at local agencies. Ask for 15 minutes of their time as a student working on a university project. Go prepared with three written questions on a single piece of paper with room to take notes:

• Could you tell me how you got started in the business?
• What are the Top 2 professional characteristics your firm looks for?
• What one thing would you suggest I do before graduation?

The next time you're out clubbing or perched on a café seat inside a world-class museum's coffee shop sipping a cappuccino with that special someone, stop and ask yourself some simple questions. "Who does the marketing for this place? Where have I seen advertising for this club? Who worked to get the article about this café placed in the Sunday Metro section?"

Buy the Sunday edition of *The Dallas Morning News* or Miami's *el Nuevo Herald*. Turn on your communication eyes. Don't read the retail ads, tally up column inches. When you see a two-page ad that jumps the gutter using a great creative visual, make a note to find the agency or in-house team that pulled off this arresting visual. A local business profile (complete with an engaging photo of the owner) means someone is working their fingers off pitching stories with a great photographer's eye.

Very few industries give their winners public visibility every day. Be glad you're not a Perl programmer whose best work will never be in plain sight.

4. **READ, READ, READ... EVERY DAY.**
Why: A communications revolution is underway.

Speak Clearly, Concisely and Convincingly

Just as you will do on every assignment you receive once you get started in the business.

Keep your vision wide, but develop a few sentences that clearly and simply state why someone should hire you. How can the person interviewing you for a position possibly know the answer to this question unless you tell them? They can't. So you tell them. Part II offers a way to tackle this task.

Relax. There is no single answer to why someone should hire you. But you do need to begin formulating the pieces of an answer. These are the characteristics, accomplishments, skills and motivation you mold into a summary of your accumulated academic and business experiences. Some people refer to it as an "elevator speech" that can be delivered in the time it takes to ride three floors up or down. Others refer to it as your "story angle." Some might even call it your "unique selling point."

You just need several honest, true, heartfelt and passionate sentences to string together in an interview. You don't need the answer to the ultimate question of life.

Think "Client-Side"

Include clients in your thinking.

Consider the following. Inside every client organization is someone who sets the communications strategy, determines the budget and then manages a wide variety of external business relationships. This includes managing the activities of advertising agencies, public relations firms, research firms, printers, trade show and event coordinators, reporters and editors from the media, regulatory and government agencies, and non-profit and charitable organizations. Plus, someone inside every company is responsible for the internal and external communications within and among the firm's own product managers, R&D, manufacturing, purchasing, operations, HR, sales, and information technology groups.

And that's only a partial list.

If you have a personal interest in a particular industry or business sector, expand your thinking to include them in your future. Pebble Beach has a marketing director. The Baltimore Orioles organization markets itself. The Lance Armstrong Foundation has an obligation to make itself known. Increasingly, state and local government entities must market themselves to their key publics.

Are you beginning to get the idea?

Use your fingers. There are many more clients than there are advertising and public relations firms. Following your passion — where motivation is easy to generate — means opening your options to include the client-side of the business equation.

Don't Forget the Media Industry

Consider the media as a career destination. Radio, network and cable television, the feature film and entertainment distribution business, local and national newspapers and magazines, the Internet, trade shows and even new media, however you choose to define that, are all in the midst of a revolution.

Who else more than the media needs your youth, current perspective and understanding of emerging audiences?

Who needs your training in the language and methods of advertising and public relations more than the media itself?

Who else could benefit most from your ability to communicate to and work effectively with public relations practitioners, media buyers and copywriters?

Don't overlook the media.

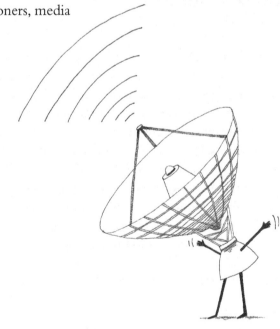

Before you plunge in deeper, steady yourself. Then be prepared to accept subtle shifts in attitude that will quickly reshape your fundamental approach to job hunting. It's a changed world and a new approach is required. But it's not Mars.

Take a Deep Breath

• You are prepared to enter the business.

You are academically ready, mentally focused. You have a demonstrated passion for advertising and public relations, and you can set aside the fear of nonconformity you've unknowingly acquired over the past 16 years.

• Understand the role that applied background research plays.

Everything you do to prepare for an interview is applied background research: Printing and highlighting pages from an agency's web site, shopping for the product sold by an agency's top client to gain a consumer perspective, or subscribing to a weekly online newsletter about new trends in search technology. The list is almost endless and limited only by your ingenuity and drive.

This type of research demonstrates your command of the business to the decision-maker. It's concrete evidence that you walk-the-walk and don't just talk-the-talk. It concurrently maintains your focus and widens your scope (a very neat trick). It is the core of your interview preparation and interview follow-up, because it empowers frequent contact with your interviewer.

• Realize that networks work.

Networks are not "who you know." Networks are "who you trust."

Recognize that trust is little more than the expectation someone will perform in a certain way. Knowing someone isn't enough. Knowing they'll follow through on their commitments is.

Your most recent network connections were probably forged during class projects, volunteer committee work and team presentations. These threads of trust accumulate throughout your academic career. Some are thin and tenuous. Others are strengthened by repeatedly working together in several classes.

Trust is built one thread at a time through performance and, amazingly enough, it sometimes takes only one thread to get you started.

• Do the work.

Do more than read and write and plan. Start now and perform the very hard work required by Your Plan. Don't stop. Persistence and tenacity are required traits in the business of advertising and public relations. If you can execute Your Plan, you will succeed in the business, because they are one and the same.

• Change your entire job-hunting perspective.

Shift from an inward-focused perspective to one focused on a decision-maker who is short-handed, pressed for time and needs a quick solution. You must devote enormous amounts of effort to gain 15 minutes of face time with this person. Then adopt the perspective that it's your job to help this decision-maker succeed at their job, even though you don't work for them. Yet.

SAND TRAPS – PAY ATTENTION AND AVOID
- Moving home to a safe place to look for a job
- Thinking New York (or Minneapolis) is too big for you
- Listening to your parents, bless their hearts
- Listening to anyone who's not working at this as hard as you are

Think You've Got...
No power? This book's method gives you some.

No contacts? This method shows you how to get a few, then grow them in number.

No time? This method says, "OK, start now" and use your time wisely.

No money? This method utilizes what you do have a lot of – brains, problem-solving skills and the ability to read and write.

5. **WHEN ENTERTAINING CLIENTS, YOU ORDER FIRST.**
Why: Quickly sets the tone for the meal.

It doesn't get much cheaper than that.

No idea what you want to do for the rest of your life? This method doesn't care about the rest of your life. It gives you a way to get started, so you can join the rest of us as we all find the answer to that Big Question.

Along the way, threaded inside the chapters, are practical business tips, advice for ways to move past stumbling blocks and some encouraging words.

Ready? Here we go.

PART II
Let's Get Started

You can skip around the chapters in this section and do just fine. Chapters 5 and 6 are the heart of this book. They offer the most important insights, because they spring from an exchange with two rather remarkable students.

Given that degree of relevance to your current state, I suggest you pay particular attention to them.

5. Katiescope

As you begin this chapter, please understand there are people in line ahead of you. They figured out what's contained in this book two or three years ago, or they used another method to get started in the business. Don't be discouraged. There is room for you. People drop by the wayside all the time, and those who survive and thrive are important to you. You'll encounter that thought again in another chapter.

Right now, the "Katiescope" and "Greg Audit" are tools to help place you near the front of the hiring line.

Put Yourself Under

So what's a Katiescope? A powerful self-assessment tool, the Katiescope is named for a very astute student who helped crystallize the concept. Imagine a giant microscope where your guts get smeared on a glass slide and then inspected. It has two levels of magnification: High and Low. The Katiescope allows you to work on both levels. High Magnification serves one function; Low Magnification serves an entirely different function. Both are required.

At each magnification level, you create lists, do research, compile information and ultimately wind up with two stacks of paper in front of you. That's the easy part. The demanding, but rewarding, part comes as you begin drawing connections between the two stacks.

• Katiescope High Magnification Overview

This is not an esteem-building exercise. Putting yourself under the Katiescope differs from introspection or self-reflection. A Katiescope requires a professional point of view in addition to a personal point of view. It requires honesty, confidence, frankness and the ability to spell out the unvarnished truth about your demonstrated performance throughout college and elsewhere.

Don't be put off by the glass slide analogy. In all likelihood, you're much too hard on yourself at this point in your career. You think the talent pool in the advertising and public relations industries is rich, deep and wide. You can't see how you fit into the overall picture. Katiescoping on High Magnification addresses that very issue.

6. **WRITE CALL REPORTS AND SEND CLIENT A COPY.**
Why: Basis for decisions and post-mortem audit trail.

• Katiescope Low Magnification Overview

Katiescoping on Low Magnification includes a significant amount of applied background research surrounding the very core of your job search. Don't interpret "Low" as less important. It's not.

This type of research is something you've probably overlooked or skimmed over. It's something that can tell you a lot about an agency you want to work for. It's something you may think is proprietary and secret, but it isn't.

This Low Magnification involves researching job descriptions, but not just any job descriptions. These job descriptions are for positions you feel you're qualified for, plus a few you feel you're not yet qualified for, but aspire to be.

Katiescope – High Magnification

Clean slate thinking coupled with a cold, scrupulous inspection of your resumé is required here. Don't mix the two. Tackle each task on separate days.

Start with a Fresh Legal Pad

Write down what you like, what you do well, what classes you liked, what topics interest you, what positive traits people use to describe you to others, what's personally motivating, and what you would do if magically every job in the world paid the same and you could live anywhere.

High Magnification includes your skills, your experience, your passion, your academic training, your interests, your natural talent, things you've been recognized for and skills, such as proficiency in certain software.

This list also should include intangibles, like your relaxed and convincing demeanor in team presentations, the fact you relish the chance to present instead of dreading the prospect, that you know how to break the ice with anyone in any social setting. It also includes things you are passionate about — military history, teaching low-income children to swim, a Triple-A ball club, the 1970s or Collings® guitars. What gets your blood up?

Put everything and anything on the High Magnification list. In any form. This is not the place to exclude thoughts; this is not the time to be selective. It doesn't matter how you articulate items. As a matter of fact, these descriptions will morph a dozen times as you re-inspect the list. Nothing is permanent at this point.

But it must be written down. No exceptions. As things pop up afterward, write them down, too. Dare to repeat the same thing already on the list from an earlier session. This is your property. Do with it as you will.

Then to the side of each item, out in the margin, whenever the urge strikes you, answer two questions: "Why is that?" and "So what?"

Turn the Knob to Sharpen the Focus

Pull out your resumé. Inspect each job or experience and describe exactly what you really did on the job. No exaggerations. No buzz words. Just the honest, unvarnished truth.

Then list awards, achievements, recognitions and top-line performance review comments from your supervisors and managers. Write everything down, including little things. Most importantly, quantify things when possible. If you were promoted in three months when it took other people six months to achieve the same thing, write that down. If you were recognized as the No. 2 sales person for a particular month, put that down. These little achievement nuggets communicate a lot in very few words, which is exactly what you want.

Finally, it's very important that you name names. Name the accounts you worked on during internships. Don't use generic descriptions! Brand names have weight. They're vivid and rich. They're detailed. As people read resumés, their eyes are drawn to brand names. Use this to your advantage. Your interviewer's agency might have an account in that same industry.

If your experience is with a local firm, include a five- to seven-word caption alongside the firm's name: "The Wiggle Room — Central Texas' leading vermiculture facility." If you interview in another city, the interviewer will need a sense of the firm you worked for to put your experience into perspective, even if it is a worm farm and bait shop.

7. **WALK AROUND; SAY HELLO; DON'T INTERRUPT LONG.**
Why: Learn the business at ground level.

You now have two High Magnification Katiescope documents. Both should be completely marked up with notes in the margins and stray words everywhere. Nothing is carved in stone. But at some point, the truth about you will start to peek through.

Tackle this High Magnification task in more than one sitting.

Katiescope – Low Magnification

Don't be fooled by the "Low Magnification" title. This is the most grinding, grueling and mind-numbing applied background research you'll ever do. So much so that you'll be tempted to cut things short. Don't. Shortcuts will limit your fuel and you're going to need a lot of fuel on this trip. Take heart, though. You'll only have to climb this hill once, so the pain passes quickly.

Do the following seven things:

1. Top 5 Agencies

Choose five advertising agencies or public relations firms you want to interview with and compile a list of their clients.

"How do I do that?"

Use http://www.redbooks.com. This site is a remarkable resource. If your college or university's main library doesn't have an unlimited subscription to redbooks.com, ask them to get one. It's a required resource. Otherwise, you'll have to work within redbooks.com's "7-day FREE TRIAL Subscription."

2. Burn your eyes and chop down trees

Visit all five agency web sites. Click through every link on every site. Yes, every link on every site. You want a job, don't you?

Read every page. Print out a fistful of pages to identify the agency's philosophy, mission, organizational structure, client roster, sample work and personality. Buy tabbed folders and file these pages by agency.

By the way, if the agency doesn't have a philosophy or mission page, this is great news. You can write one for them based on your analysis, then screw up your courage during an interview and present it to the interviewer. "What?! I can't do that!" Oh, yes you can. Oh, yes you will. My job is to help convince you this opportunity exists.

3. Five Big 3 Clients

Visit the web sites of each agency's three largest clients. Bookmark those URLs, moving each bookmark into a separate folder you've created for each of your five target agencies.

Start reading. Find and print out each client's "Site Map." This text-only page typically gives you a high-elevation view of the firm in one long page. It's often organized in a way that clearly illustrates how each client sees itself and, in turn, presents itself to the world. This can be a handy thing to know.

4. Hi/Lo

Hi – Repeat the bookmarking process, but this time add another set of client URLs to each agency's folder. Add the agency's client URLs you like or think might be fun to work on.

Lo – Do the same thing at the other end of the spectrum. Bookmark the accounts that are likely to be ones that no one in the agency clamors to work on, like "Multi-viscosity, industrial lubricants." In essence, you are building a Hi/Lo client list for each agency.

5. Industry Sectors

List the industry sectors that cover all of the clients for all five agencies. For example, banking, retail clothing, agricultural manufacturing, lighting and flooring, hospitals and non-profits.

Now dig three layers deep into industry sectors:

The Trade — Use your favorite search site to find the leading trade association for each sector. Do the same to find the leading trade publication that reports industry news. Do the same to find the primary industry trade show for each sector.

Bookmark these URLs. Are you getting the point?

For banking, there's the American Bankers Association. Its news publication is the American Banker, a daily newspaper that every banker in the U.S. reads daily. On the trade show side, there's the "Bank Marketing Annual Convention" that usually takes place in one of the top leisure destination cities in the country.

http://www.aba.com/
http://www.americanbanker.com/
http://www.aba.com/bankmarketing/

Every client has a trade association. Every client has an industry news publication. Every client has a big trade show. You need to know all of these names.

Annual Reports and Analyst Reports — For publicly traded firms, read each client's annual report. Go online to a popular brokerage firm site. Read one of their stock analyst's sector reports and specific reports on the client. This is a great way to get a condensed, business point of view on the client and their competition.

Know the client's closing stock price yesterday. This tells you if the client is happy or besieged.

Street — Hit the pavement. Go buy the product, take a test drive or request a free sample. Do something smart at the street level. Visit a client's retail store or go shopping at Wal-Mart® to see how consumers encounter the product in the aisle. Visit the client's corporate headquarters: Walk in, look around, pick up a brochure, take a tour. It's virtually guaranteed that none of the people you're interviewing against will have done this.

Then visit the client's biggest competitor's headquarters and do the same.

Feeling comfortable with the clients and their sectors? That's the idea.

6. Open Positions

Visit all five agency web sites again. This time, focus your attention on finding, reading and printing every job description for every position open at each of your Top 5 Agencies.

It's OK to play over your head here; no one will know or care. Read descriptions that say things like, "1-3 years experience," "must have supervisory experience" and "experience with user interface design." Or "DART®/DFA, SRDS®, MRI®, Atlas®, Nielsen//NetRatings®," or "Cision®" or "NetView Usage Metrics®." Whatever.

Print these out and drop them into your agency folders.

Since jobs open and are filled all the time, it makes sense to revisit each agency's site periodically.

7. Job Descriptions

Print out a dozen job descriptions for a dozen different positions from a dozen agencies – excluding your Top 5 Agencies.

Visit the web sites of major agencies in major markets. Do some serious applied research.

Now you are free to go to monster.com or any other online job site. Don't get sucked into the ease of use, volume of results, and sense of power and control these sites are very adept at conveying.

As the song "Smuggler's Blues" says, "It's the lure of easy money; it's got a very strong appeal."

8. **LEARN TO THUMB TYPE.**
Why: Increase productivity during travel time.

Your objective is to assemble a stack of 20 to 50 job descriptions, then begin tearing each one apart, bit by bit. You're looking for phrases and requirements that are, amazingly enough, repeated across job descriptions, regardless of which firm is advertising for the position. The more you read, the more you are able to pick out the truly unique elements of each job description.

You are "calibrating" job descriptions. You dial out the generic language that peppers every job description. These phrases and "requirements" are being copied and pasted from an HR Job Description Manual. They're included because the agency wants to be industry standard and compliant.

Reading widely also enables you to identify unique phrases inserted by the manager with whom you hope to interview. Or, they've been inserted by someone in the agency who has been swamped with applicants after posting a generic job description. This is what you're looking for. Once you get into the rhythm, you can pluck out the subtle differences that distinguish various job descriptions.

More Is Better

Whoa! Do you have to do *all* of this? No. But the more you do, the better. You are trying to push your way through the interviewer's door. The more prepared you are when that door swings open, the better the conversation you can have on the other side.

Remember, the person you're trying to interview with has done all of this and more. As you approach this level of preparation, you increase the chance of having an interesting conversation with the person who might hire you. You will have more to say, more to talk about, more opportunities to ask good questions. Plus, you demonstrate both your willingness to work and a disciplined work ethic.

Now Apply Creative Thinking

Whew – Piles of Brain Fuel

You now have five nested agency bookmark folders on your computer, with five to seven URLs in each folder.

You also have five file folders containing printouts of key pages, along with stapled collections of pages from the agency's Big 3 Clients, including the client's "Site Map" page on top.

Not only that, you have a bead on the overlapping industry sectors important to your Top 5 Agencies.

Finally, you have in your pocket at least 25 to 50 printed job descriptions, courtesy of HR departments from the industry-leading firms in advertising and public relations.

Read and Study

All of this applied research needs to be read, assimilated and digested.

Don't allow your analysis to become an abstract exercise. This isn't school. This is your time. This is infinitely more important than any other homework assignment or research project you've ever worked on.

This is the foundation of your career.

Think

Ask practical questions. Study the material in any way you see fit.

Top 5 Agencies – All is laid bare for you to see on their web sites. It's available for inspection at your leisure, conveniently printed out and ready for highlighting.

Big 3 Clients – Herein lie the seeds of your future in the form of potential news items, perhaps one of the most important and powerful tactical devices you have at your disposal. You just can't see that right now. This will become very clear later in the book.

Hi/Lo – These are opportunities. The Hi list contains accounts where your passion will effortlessly propel you. On the Lo list are tough-to-love accounts others don't want, but you would willingly take on to earn your spurs in difficult, demanding and unpopular territory.

Sectors – These bookmarks lead to relevant news sites specific to each industry sector. You may have just experienced a little "Ah-ha" moment. If so, that is very good. If not, don't worry. Dominos are about to start clicking together.

Job Descriptions – You'll gain clarity as you begin to see patterns within the words. Plus, something very important should be starting to happen. You should begin to sense where you fit in. You should glimpse yourself in these positions.

Ask Questions

In applied background research, questions are more important than answers. Nowhere is this more critical than in the dissection and study of your stack of job descriptions.

- What do people really do all day in this position?
- What are the common characteristics that run through every job description?
- Why are those "weasel words" in there? "...is a plus," "...preferred, but not required" and "...is desirable."
- What specific acronyms, buzzwords and abbreviations are required?
- Why is there so much talk about having the ability to communicate well?
- Why does the ability to work well on a team seem to be really important?
- Why do all the desirable personality traits sound very familiar?
- What's going on here?

Click

"Wait! I can do that."

Yes, you can. Yes, you will.

This is why the Katiescope High Magnification section ends with a tough look at your existing resumé. This is why accomplishments in your internships and experience are important. This also is why brand names are important in your resumé. If you can describe what you actually did on a particular job, you can read a wide variety of different job descriptions and come pretty close to understanding exactly what takes place on a job.

This calibration process is little more than becoming experienced in peeling away the standardized HR language and uncovering what really goes on inside the job you want to apply for. That's why you read a dozen job descriptions, for a dozen different positions, from a dozen agencies.

But here is the really important part: The entire process dramatically lowers your fear factor. This allows you to begin drawing parallels between job openings and your own experience, regardless of where your experience was derived.

Which is what the final Katiescoping step includes.

Draw Lines Between High Magnification and Low Magnification

This step is crucial, so take your time. Turn on your analytical skills. Turn on the creative side of your brain. They're both required to fully understand what you're about to do.

The problem is complex. Lay out your High and Low Magnification analyses so you can see everything clearly. Take up the whole floor, kitchen table or dining room table. Do whatever it takes.

The general idea is spelled out below. You are free to bend, modify, stretch, amend and generally twist the process to fit who you are.

It might go something like the following:

- Draw connections between High Magnification and Low Magnification.
- Write on the lines that connect the two.
- Add new things to both lists. Let your High Magnification list enlarge and grow after re-reading things in the Low Magnification pile. Do the reverse.
- Toward the end, you must be liberal yet honest. These connections are your selling points. They are the "reasons why" someone should consider you for a position.

Practice making these connections. Modify both lists after each interview, if that helps. Start over if necessary.

Why a Katiescope?

What You're Doing

You are transitioning from the academic world to the business world. You've just passed through the structured, very systematized, well-oiled and family-oriented American educational system. So you're pretty good at going to school.

Learning how to build a bridge from one world to another world is tough. But now you have some things going for you. All of your applied research is spread out before you. You own that. You own the insights drawn from your analyses. You own the perspectives on 15 to 25 clients. You own the sources for industry news. You own the whole thing.

9. **TRY NEW THINGS. BE A GENERALIST.**
Why: Reduces dependency on others; it's a competitive edge.

Now begin shaping the things that will come out of your mouth during interviews.

Learn how to subtly point out these connections in conversation. Practice. Practice out loud. Try delivering these connections on a variety of levels to various types of people in an agency, from a prospective team member all the way up to the agency's president. In all likelihood, you'll be talking to a wide range of people if interviews go into a second and third round.

Why You're Doing It

A Katiescope shapes your strategy. More importantly, a Katiescope shapes your perspective.

You are now almost in the business. Think about that for a second.

You know a lot about five agencies. In fact, you probably know more than most of the employees in each agency.

You know a lot about 15 or more clients. As a matter of fact, you probably have a broader perspective than some employees who work exclusively on one or two accounts inside each agency.

You know which clients get your blood pumping. You also can see the ones who probably have few champions inside the agency — which might translate into an opportunity for you during an interview.

You know about several industry sectors. You know where to quickly find news items and trend information that affects each agency's clients. During your research, you might have e-mailed a question to a trade publication columnist and received a response, which is something you could smoothly work into an interview. You can talk about the trade show in Las Vegas that everyone working on the account wants to attend.

You've cracked the code on job descriptions. You have a pretty clear picture of the important traits, key skills and intangibles that agencies are looking for in candidates.

Most importantly, you can see yourself performing well in a particular job. You are now beginning to understand yourself from the interviewer's perspective.

Now you're ready for a Greg Audit.

"I'd like to drop by your office tomorrow for a Greg audit."

That's how it started. Right before spring graduation, another very insightful student set the agenda for a meeting using those exact words. Greg wanted an assessment of his resumé to identify weak spots. He got something a bit more involved.

It has now evolved into a natural follow-on to the Katiescope, much to your benefit.

Find Someone with Scars

Find a veteran in the business with some scars on their back. It might be a faculty member or someone they recommend you visit. It could be someone you met during an internship. It certainly can include a top manager within an organization you did volunteer work for. They owe you.

You want someone who has gone through several agency reviews on either side of the equation — representing an agency or from the client-side. Even better, find someone who has seen both sides. Find someone who has hired and fired several advertising agencies and public relations firms in their career. Find someone with line responsibility who has hired and fired people. The more the better.

Ideally, this person holds you in positive regard and cares enough about you to be honest and blunt.

Schedule a 30-minute meeting with them.

Control the Agenda

Ease into the Topic

Hand them your resumé. Ask them to point out your weak spots, identify holes in your story, indicate where you need to paint things over to cover an ugly spot, and where you need to repair gaps in your story wall.

Ask them to talk about things that will make your story more stable, durable and believable.

Don't inject any additional thoughts or questions after they start talking. Don't talk any more. Don't add details. Don't defend. Don't do anything. Just listen.

Take notes. Sit quietly. Let them talk. Don't ask for clarification. Don't peck at anything that falls on the floor. Wait through long pauses. That's when insights and bruising comments emerge. You want that.

Again, don't do anything except listen and write. Say, "Thank you" when they're finished.

Close with the Heart of the Audit

Now tell this same person your four best characteristics. Better yet, well before this meeting, write these characteristics in four, short, clear sentences on a single sheet of paper. Hand your veteran that list.

Ask that they read the list and think about it for a minute.

Here comes the critical part: Ask this person to reword and play back those same four characteristics to you, but in their words, not your words. Give them plenty of time to formulate their response.

Don't add details. Don't defend. Don't do anything. Let them think. They'll start talking when they're good and ready.

When they do start talking, take copious notes. Sit silently and record exact phrasing and wording.

It may take three or four very uncomfortable, long pauses to get what you want. Give these thoughts a chance to form in your veteran's mind.

You're waiting for condensed business language to start flowing. This includes catch phrases picked up throughout their career you've never heard before. It might be a reordering of your four thoughts to reflect current best practices in the business. A simple tightening of words to register a point more quickly might pop out. A phrase might be turned or twisted to emphasize one of your accomplishments in a new way.

Please don't ask for clarification. Please don't ask them to repeat something. Please don't do anything but listen. And write. Then say, "Thank you" when they're done.

Get up and leave the room. Read and reflect on your notes.

Within your veteran's response are descriptions, phrases and wording more closely aligned to the business world than to the academic world. Tucked away in these notes are fresh ways to describe your achievements. Most importantly, these notes contain the language, ordering and emphasis that other recent graduates don't have. This sets you apart in an interview.

That's your Greg Audit. It's a hard, critical eye on "the books." It's a terse, industry-standard evaluation and a new set of words to describe your best qualities.

Whoa! Not So Fast

Greg Audits are hard to do. So recognize that not every grizzled veteran is able or willing to do this for you. If you wait patiently and nothing is forthcoming, stop.

Don't force things into an uncomfortable position with someone who is valuable to you in many other ways. Use your own good judgment. If things aren't working, find another person to help you with this task.

If the Greg Audit is going to work, it will work. If not, give the other person a graceful and diplomatic exit path.

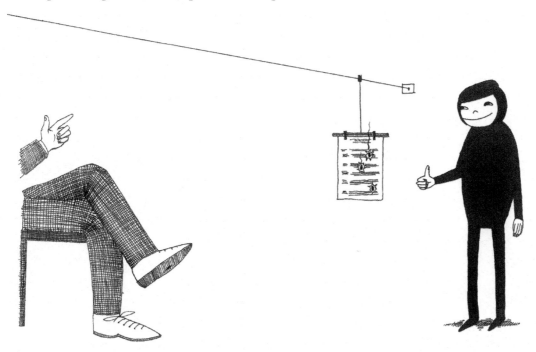

Coming off the Greg Audit, this should be a cakewalk. And it is.

Imagine That

Worry is the misuse of imagination and daydreaming is imaginary wandering. Think of the possibilities with disciplined imagination. New things happen.

Permission to Dream

Write down the title, "21 Things I Want to Do Before I Die."

Make a list.

Keep things simple. Try "verb and predicate" first. You can put the flesh on the bones later.

There's no reason to put things into any particular order. The list will change 100 times.

Don't share the list with anyone, for any reason. Take the pressure off; it's your list. It includes your dreams. It's specific to you.

This goes far beyond professional aspirations.

OK, Here's an Example

Maybe it looks something like the following:

• Teach
• Overhaul a bicycle
• Learn to sail
• Write a book
• Read *The History of The Decline and Fall of the Roman Empire* by Edward Gibbon
• Visit Mecca
• Drink Irish coffee at the Buena Vista Bar as fog rolls in under the Golden Gate Bridge

- Go coast-to-coast-to-coast by motorcycle
- Travel first class to London, then see Stonehenge at sunrise
- Invent something
- Lose 30 pounds
- Own a pair of handmade boots

Rules

There is only one rule regarding this list of 21 things: It must be written.

However, a suggestion is in order. Allocate adequate time to pull this list together. Do it all alone. You've just put four years of hard work into earning your degree. Dreams certainly deserve a day or so.

What Does This Have to Do with Finding a Job?

Finding a job is very important to you today.

Once you find that job, you'll be working some incredibly long hours, because the business is an exhilarating rush. Everyone around you is working insane hours. You'll work hard. You'll play hard. It's fun.

Then somewhere along the way, other matters begin to press into that professional world. Slowly, quietly, with irresistible force, other matters begin to nudge you gently back into balance.

Your list of "21 Things I Want to Do Before I Die" plants the seeds that will one day help you rebalance your life.

An old preacher once said, "You know, I've been at the bedsides of many of my congregation near the end of long and fruitful lives. Never once have I heard a single person say, 'I wish I'd spent more time at the office.'"

Keep this in mind as you begin your career. Figure out how you order the following things:

- Your health
- Your family
- Your faith
- Your friends

• Your profession
• Your community

From time to time, these shuffle about. But don't let the business
drive the order. Take care.

The initial focal point for Your Plan is your resumé. More precisely, the initial focal point for Your Plan is your *modular* resumé.

So create a base resumé that can be quickly tailored to a specific interview. This base resumé contains all of your core messaging.

To be most effective, you must modify your resumé to appeal specifically to the decision-maker who will decide whether to interview you or not.

A Dozen Mechanical Things

1. It's an ad.

Your resumé is a one-page ad with a single, focused and strategic objective. It must motivate someone to call you in for an interview. That's it.

2. Do your homework.

Read the research you've done on the agency and the decision-maker you're about to contact. Refresh yourself on the agency's web site. Print out pages. Highlight things and take notes. Prepare for a test. If you go into this test unprepared, it's not just a bad grade. You won't get the interview.

3. Write to an audience of one.

Your modular resumé should be a unique piece directed specifically to one person.

Vary the content of each section based on the sum total of your applied research. If the company is an aggressive, cutting-edge firm whose web site pushes creative boundaries, then skew your language in that direction. If the firm's web site describes its strengths as "a global, integrated communications leader helping Fortune™ 100 corporations navigate the treacherous waters ahead,"

you might want to tone it down and take a more conservative approach.

4. Objectives are specific to your audience.

If you decided to include an "Objectives" section (it's not recommended you do this), you must make the objectives specific to the agency you're interviewing with.

Get focused. Be proactive and assertive. Be honest. Don't be humble.

If you're a copywriter with a passion for writing, say so.

> "I'm a copywriter who's ready to write compelling copy for every assignment Tribal DDB Dallas gives me, small or large. I'm ready to pay my dues, because at the end of that period, I'm going to be the one left standing with a great portfolio of collateral pieces, brochures and small space ads that worked. I'm ready to earn my way up to plum assignments."

Objectives tell what you'll *do for* the decision-maker, not what you want from them.

Soft objectives, such as "I want a position in which I can apply my skills and learn how the entire advertising process works," are a mistake. It tells the reader you're still in learning mode, you're still in school and you're not ready to build on the strong academic preparation you've paid dearly for.

Figure out what you accomplished in your internships. Figure out what you like to do. Build objectives that tell the reader what you can do for their clients.

5. Use verb/predicate bullet lists judiciously.

Bulleted lists are quick jabs. But they have to land to do any good.

A series of "• Presented to…" and "• Pulled my weight in…" etc. can be effective. Avoid dull wording and don't use the same verbs and descriptors your competitors use. Stand out with your own choice of words.

Then break out of the mold. Write a three-sentence paragraph that has energy and life and speaks the truth. Give your interviewer some relief.

10. **RETURN PHONE CALLS IMMEDIATELY.**
Why: Nothing's ruder than postponing a return call.

6. Write copy that sings.

Start fires with your words. Use active verbs. Name names. Articulate your accomplishments, not job duties. The difference is significant.

- Internships
  - Two are required; more are better.
  - Brand-name firms are better than unknown firms.
  - Vary what you say about each; these forays remove "gee-whiz" from your voice.
  - Internships reduce the number of "false starts," that is, learning you don't like the advertising or public relations business during your first job.

- Summer Jobs
  - Summer jobs in or closely related to advertising and public relations are best.
  - Jobs closely related to the agency's biggest client are good.
  - Name the accounts you worked on; spell out the nature of the firm if its name isn't nationally known.

- Achievements
  - Quantified achievements are vivid and memorable.
  - Generic achievements are harmful; they put you in bad company.

7. You can't say everything.

Resumés are not a plodding, chronological listing of your work history to prove you're going to be a loyal comrade in the assembly line of life.

Ads don't do that. Why should your resumé? Remember: Your resumé is an ad. Pull out your unique selling propositions; you have more than one. Find the consumer benefit where the consumer is an agency manager you want to work for. Be selective. Focus on your strengths. Twist your weaknesses around with a realistic point of view statement.

Avoid going back to the beginning of time. A reference to something done before college signals a lack of current and relevant experiences, or nostalgia for a lost world. Both are damaging.

If you include a "Personal Interests" section, make it compelling,

11. **PREPARE A WRITTEN AGENDA FOR YOUR MEETINGS.**
Why: Gives you total control over the meeting.

provocative, surprising and uniquely you. Any other tepid content is a waste of space.

8. One page.

One page. No exceptions.

9. Multiple languages are a big deal.

If you are fluent in more than one language, you are the future of advertising and public relations. Please don't hide that fact at the bottom of the page with a "Fluent in Spanish" statement.

Elevate this. Write a strategically intriguing sentence in Spanish. If the reader can understand it, you've just scored a point. If they have to have it translated, you score a point when the translator reads it and you score another point when they read it out loud to the person who asked for the translation. If they can't read it and feel threatened to the point that they mention it in an interview, tell them to hire you pronto to solve the problem.

10. Vary the density of your content.

Avoid writing six sections all of the same length. Add visual variety.

Use word counts to emphasize a section's importance. Maybe one section contains only one sentence. If it's a great sentence, so be it.

11. Lay out the page.

Think about white space. Don't forget things like call-out columns. Place key elements in italics. Use indentations. Center a copy block, then draw attention to it with triple spacing.

Finally, thumbtack your resumé to a wall. Walk away 10 feet. Turn around and look at it. Is it distinctive? Or does it look like everyone else's?

12. Demonstrate your command of advertising and public relations on one page.

A modular resumé enables you to talk about the strategy behind your resumé, in addition to the content within your resumé. It's OK to talk about why you organized your resumé in a certain way for a particular interview.

As a matter of fact, this can be a defining difference between you and your competitors. If you are able to explain the strategy behind this creative piece of work – your resumé – then you can do the same for a print ad, radio script, 30-second spot storyboard or web site.

It's a valuable skill to already have mastered.

WHAT REALLY HAPPENS TO YOUR RESUMÉ

The decision-maker is overworked and under pressure to fill the slot quickly so productivity can resume. They will handle the hiring task at the end of a very long day when they're tired and want to go home. The process looks something like the following:

It's 6:20 p.m.
Need to be home by 7:30 p.m. to even hope to see my family before bedtime.
HR screened the resumé pile down to the 70 sitting in front of me.
Make two stacks: Keepers and Rejects.
Scan the first one for experience, brand names and buzz words.
Four seconds later, do the same to the next resumé.
Don't read details – the good ones will jump out of the stack.
Completely ignore the ones that even look as though the content is thin.
Read bullet points to pick up the pace, it's getting late.
Forget the ones with dense text, there's no time to dig stuff out of that pile.
A typo? Auto-Reject. Don't even skim it. That's easy.

It's 6:45 p.m.
The Keeper stack has 24, that's 16 too many.
Work the Keeper stack.
Highlight agency names, client names and specific skills or software.
Cull the ones who didn't point out what they achieved or were recognized for.
I wonder what he really did on that project?
Find one well-written sentence or phrase that has a spark of energy.
They all look alike. Did everyone read the same "How to" book?

It's 6:55 p.m.
Down to a stack of nine.
Invite six to come in next week knowing not everyone will be able to make it.
Cut three, but sit on them in case we hit a dead end with the finalists.
Can only interview four to five – the team gets burned out and loses interest.
These six look OK.
Photocopy the six, route them to the team and get some feedback.

It's 7:10 p.m.
I'm going to be late.

Follow Rules Only When Required to Do So

Now that you know what really happens to your resumé, don't get discouraged. Use this insight to understand that you must satisfy two people — your decision-maker and their HR department. This requires you to adhere to the firm's HR rules, but stay 100% focused on the person making the hiring decision.

Only the decision-maker counts. Once you've broken through and earned their attention, it's up to them to instruct you on what rules to follow. Stick to those rules religiously, but never abandon your efforts to maintain a high level of interaction with the decision-maker.

• Again, HR plays a vital, necessary role in the job-interview process to meet the regulatory and legal obligations that protect the agency from lawsuits. But HR doesn't know the reality of the job you're interviewing for.

• The decision-maker is a department manager who makes this hiring decision in consultation with their agency team, because the team has to work with and get along with you on a daily basis.

• Your strategy is to minimize interaction with HR, while at the same time, make contact with the right decision-maker. Unfortunately for you, in a job-hunting situation there are a number of agency employees paid and motivated to protect the decision-maker from the likes of you. Be prepared to be persistent and pushy.

If this sounds somewhat like a "client-agency" relationship, it should. Your job is to manage your way in, make a great pitch and win the business.

Interview Game Plan

To do this, you must first attract the attention of the right decision-maker. Then do whatever it takes to get a 15-minute conversation with that person. In the last minute of the interview, you politely ask for permission to maintain contact. Then maintain high-quality, frequent contact after the interview.

Do this again and again to demonstrate your professional skills. As long as the follow-up benefits the decision-maker, and *never* falls into the category of begging for a job, you continue.

10 MINUTES EARLY IS LATE

15 MINUTES EARLY If your interviewer is ready to start, you'll get more face time.

14 MINUTES EARLY You can look around and judge the office mood by simple observation.

13 MINUTES EARLY You see who leaves in a huff, with a smile, or muttering obscenities.

12 MINUTES EARLY Notice how your interviewer uses the time between meetings. It's an important cue.

11 MINUTES EARLY You'll glance at your watch and start to worry about being late.

10 MINUTES EARLY You're late.

Push Your Research into the Light, and Keep It There

You may have to grab the reins at some point in the interview.

You can't do an enormous amount of applied research then allow it to lie around. It does you no good if it's hidden in your head and you forget to mention it, or aren't given an easy opportunity to mention it.

It's your job to figure out how to get this research up and on the table, even if it means saying, "Thank you very much. Before you introduce me to the rest of the team, could we talk about something interesting I found while preparing for this interview? I think you may find it valuable."

You add value at this point in the job-hunting process by giving away your brains a little bit at a time: Giving away a creative idea, an insight about a competitor, a key audience statistic, a strategic media mix idea or a high-impact public relations concept a firm used in Canton, Ohio.

This also is the basis for your high-quality, frequent contact after the interview. You will never be perceived as a pest, an unwanted caller, an irritating interruption or a job stalker if you keep this idea and point of view in mind.

You are helping someone else succeed at their job. And yes, you're working for free. That's the price of admission into the business.

LOOK LIKE YOU MEAN IT Carry a legal- or letter-sized writing portfolio when you interview. Why?

- It makes you look professional.
- It offers a convenient place to keep your business cards at hand.
- It lets you easily take notes.
- It's a way to carry around your applied research.
- It's a business-like place to store the materials your interviewer gives you.
- It also gives you something to do with your hands.

Tell Them

Build a "tell-them-what-you-told-them" speech. Do this so they don't miss your strategy, your preparation and your demonstrated passion. Sometimes your interviewer is too distracted or too tired to pay close attention. Sometimes they don't have time to pause and recognize your strategy. It's OK to tell them what you're doing and why you're doing it.

It might sound something like this:

"I just demonstrated in a concrete way my passion to work for you and win this job with my...

...online research skills."
(printed, highlighted pages and my head full of key facts)

...practical, street-level research skills."
(visited the client and purchased their product)

...organizational skills."
(by having a written list of questions — yours and mine)

...account service skills."
(give these three photocopies to your client)

...assertiveness, initiative and proactive client approach."
(for example, right now)

...ability to be a team player."
(by telling you exactly what I'm up to)

"If this is what you're looking for, then I'd like to continue this conversation at a new level."

"If this isn't what you're looking for, let's talk some more and define your criteria."

The 15-Minute Rule

You must smoothly attempt to end your interview after exactly 14 minutes. Hopefully, you'll be restrained by the interviewer, but if not, leave after 15 minutes.

In your follow-up efforts, remind your interviewer that you kept your word. You stuck to your 15-minute deadline.

Here comes the scary part. This is the bridge between your preparation and getting an interview. One interview. It's the first test of Your Plan, your preparation and you.

Landing your first interview is an intimidating, irritating and sometimes frustrating task. The whole interview process is new and uncomfortable. Not only that, since the stakes are very high and very personal, there's a layer of intensity and stress surrounding the whole thing.

It also may seem as though the process is somewhat chaotic and filled with sheer happenstance. People get jobs by walking in off the street. Others work hard, yet it takes three to six months to land a job. One minute, agencies are hiring like crazy; the next minute, no one will talk to you.

Informational Interviews Aren't

An "information only" interview isn't. That sentence is correct. Read it again, please.

An informational interview is an opportunity. It's an opportunity to get in front of a decision-maker for 15 minutes. It's an opportunity to use your lead-in, your 15 minutes of face time and your interview follow-up to demonstrate your passion, skills and abilities.

Your objective is to surprise and delight the interviewer, then follow up with permission. It's why you did your applied research. It's why you have a modular resumé.

However, you've also heard the old saying, "The best way to kill a bad product is to advertise it well." The same is true for informational interviews. If you misuse them, word will get around very, very quickly.

Wishful Thinking

Right about now, the orderly, step-by-step HR route may start to look pretty good. Online job sites promising thousands of job openings are sounding better and better. "Come in and fill out a form." "Submit your resumé to hundreds of potential employers at the touch of a button." It all sounds very straightforward and business-like. It appears as though it's an orderly way to fairly assess candidates and ensure "the best person" wins the job.

But it's not. It's a thundering herd. It's the computer-mediated parsing of your digitized resumé in a quest for keywords.

Stay Focused

You got into the advertising and public relations fields because you like people. You pursued a career in communications because you were good at it before you entered college. You've just finished a challenging, rewarding and exhausting academic regimen. If you're on track with the method proposed in this book, you're facing an incredible amount of focused, background research. But it's not enough.

You need an interview. To be perfectly blunt, you need one interview at one of your Top 5 Agencies.

This chapter explains how to do that. First, by pointing out some practical realities about networks. Next, by convincing you that it's OK to ask for help, even if you feel this is a sign of weakness or immaturity. Finally, this chapter spells out exactly what you want your network to do for you.

Why Networks Are Particularly Important in Advertising and Public Relations

Face facts. The advertising and public relations business is a relatively small, very efficient, service industry. Because of its magnetic pull, entry-level professionals accept low starting salaries just to break into the business. But the work is very demanding and stressful. Not everyone is cut out for it. People drop out of the business all the time.

When you combine the constant salary suppression at entry-level positions with the attrition rate among those with two or three years of experience, the situation boils down to frequent job hopping. In a very practical sense, this means that advertising professionals must jump from agency to agency to achieve meaningful salary increases and additional job responsibilities.

The whole process tends to be quite robust and, not coincidentally, contributes to a very competitive, cutthroat business climate.

12. **ALWAYS ATTACK.**
Why: Someone will tell you to stop. If not, attack again.

Amazingly enough, this process works in your favor. And it all revolves around networks of people.

How so? Everyone in the business seems to know everyone else. It's partially true. The business is small. People in the business worked alongside their competitors early in their career at entry-level jobs in the same agency.

In an ideal world, you know someone who knows someone in one of your Top 5 Agencies. This is why internships are so valuable. It also is likely that someone on the faculty in the department you're graduating from has industry experience or stays in touch with alumni in the business. If so, life is very good, because both are potential starting points for your network. If not, it's of no consequence. You will quickly overcome this by directly approaching a key decision-maker in one of your Top 5 Agencies.

Face-to-Face Interaction

Before jumping into the meat of this network section, a word of caution is required. It's required because of the time you're reading this book. You are living in the midst of some revolutionary changes taking place in personal communications. Because of this, you have a distorted view of networks. You are very adaptive and comfortable using technology to create entirely new forms of networks. This is one of your biggest strengths and it's why you are so desirable to agencies. It's also a potential weakness.

Peer-to-peer, you're extremely comfortable using e-mail, social networking web sites, blogs, IM and cell phones to take care of important personal tasks. As a matter of fact, you like those communication tools because they give you some distance. These tools give you a measure of control over both time and place, and shield you from the vagaries and complications inherent in face-to-face interactions.

But understand: Your networking must be done one-on-one and face-to-face.

You cannot operate under the illusion that e-mail, phone calls, letters or small group settings will suffice. They don't. This is personal. This is business. This is when looking someone in the eye is required.

There is no substitute for personal conversation. None.

Why? Because of your audience. The person making a decision about whether or not to hire you is at least a full generation or two behind you in their mindset regarding communications and technology. That's an important fact you must recognize and utilize. These managers entered the business several years ago and have been seasoned under old, personal communication methods. To believe that your interviewer embraces and utilizes technology as deeply and fluidly as you do is a mistake.

Advertising and public relations are face-to-face businesses for some very good reasons, not the least of which is trust underpins everything.

Networks

There are several obvious things about networks worth repeating.

1. Networks work and you need one.

2. A network is not "who you know." A network is "who you trust."

3. Networks are empowering.

You currently have a network firmly in place. But your haste is blinding you to its existence and utility. You also might think you have the wrong kind of network. Or, that your network isn't big enough. That's OK, too. There's a way to overcome that.

You can build a network if you think about it, create a plan and then work Your Plan. It takes creative thinking. It takes focus. It takes time.

Remember, networks don't happen overnight.

Threads of Trust

Stretch your imagination a bit. Think of trust as being a single strand of a spider's web. Networks are a collection of these threads. At the end of your academic career, these strands have been forged in countless class projects, during internships, in student committees, on summer jobs or while doing volunteer work.

These strands are nothing more, and certainly nothing less, than performance under stress. It's knowing who you can count on: The classmates who pulled their weight on team projects, the one who would help you polish PowerPoint® slides the night before a presentation, the ones who stayed up and helped assemble the final written report at 3 a.m.

You also remember from your internships who got tired and left early. You remember the person who didn't have their materials ready on deadline and you had to pick up the slack. You know who complained a lot and constantly made excuses.

One at a Time
Spider webs are built on single strands of thread, made one connection at a time. In advertising and public relations, that translates to one contact point at a time.

These contact points are very difficult to forge, but they gain in strength as they accumulate. They are remarkably durable over time and reap great rewards when handled with care.

Network strands are thin connective threads, not thick ropes. Individually, they are easily broken. Cumulatively, they are nearly impossible to break.

This is how frequency comes into play with networks. Remember that thought.

Get Close
Work the leads where you have a recent connection — a class project client, an internship, a volunteer obligation or on the job.

Fewer Is Better
Minimize the number of out-of-the-blue, "Hi, remember me?" attempts. Those are hard on you, and very hard on the person at the other end of the conversation. They can work, but they require a lot more effort to pull off. You'll learn more about this in a few moments.

Throw Lines Out
Your strategy is a one-thread-at-a-time, spread-over-time strategy. Let them build up, even though this sounds incredibly dull and stupid right now.

You believe there's no time. You'll starve before it works. Someone else will get the job. They'll forget you. They won't even call you back.

Misguided thinking. Throw out lines one thread at a time. Then sit back and watch the web form.

Borrow One
Sometimes, someone will offer you a thread if you ask for it.

Learning to ask is part of the business. If you've earned it, if your resumé plants the seed or a great interview conversation leads to it... ask for help.

It might sound something like this:

> Them: "We don't have a position open right now. But your resumé is impressive and I appreciate how well prepared you were for today's interview, especially the media plan you brought with you from your last team project."

> You: "Thank you. I understand and will stay in contact with you and continue to demonstrate how much I want to work for Carter Design.

> "I believe I could quickly contribute to your Carter Design team, but I also know if I have some experience working at another agency whose work you value, I could make another run for a position here.

> "Based on our conversation today and what you pointed out as my strong points, may I ask if there is anyone else in the business you think I should talk to?

> "May I have one of your business cards so I can stay in touch?"

These aren't the best words. And the person may not be comfortable enough to refer you to a colleague in another firm. But these words convey what most professionals would recognize as a diplomatic yet assertive way to get an additional interview opportunity.

Or in other words, it would demonstrate your belief that you're already in the business, even though you don't have an agency job. Yet.

Attitude counts.

Champions
You only need one or two.

Understand the need to have someone who believes in you during the job-search process. Someone who does a little cheerleading for you every now and then. Someone who's on your side. They're out there, so ask for help. Then listen and lean.

Finding a job in advertising and public relations can be a tough road. So it's perfectly OK to accept a cold bottle of water along the way. As a matter of fact, it's required. Graciously accepting gifts is an art that benefits both the giver and the receiver. Learn how to do this, even if it doesn't come naturally.

Choose wisely. The people best suited for this are probably not the people who know you best. They are too protective. They care too much. More importantly, they don't know the business.

The word "mentor" might pop into your mind. But mentors generally evolve over relatively long, stable business relationships. Instead, inspect your internships. Did someone seem genuinely interested in seeing you succeed? Did anyone offer to help you break into the business? Did someone listen to your thoughts and ideas? That's the person you want to reconnect with.

Don't be shy. Everyone is hard pressed for time and stretched thin. You'll need to refresh and remind them, then politely, assertively and diplomatically demand their attention. If the person at the other end is the right kind of person, they'll remember how difficult it was to get started and slow down long enough to give you a hand.

Someone who graduated six months or a year ahead of you is perfectly capable of being a champion. Don't overlook this possibility. You can't lean very hard on them though, because they're working 10 to 15 hours a day, six days a week, trying to establish their own track record. But they'll slow down and lend you a little hand. They were, after all, in your situation not long ago.

Just keep in mind that relationships are built one thread at a time through performance. Sometimes it only takes one string to get started.

"Hi, Remember Me?"

These are difficult to pull off. But it may be where you're standing right now, so it's an option.

Make the phone call. With some authority, here's how the conversation might play out:

> You: "Hello Mr. Grant, this is Bob Jones. You may not remember me, but I was an account services intern two years ago."

13. **WORK FROM A WRITTEN JOB DESCRIPTION AND ANNUAL GOALS.**
Why: Tells you what you are paid to do. Did you win or lose?

Them: "Hello, Bob. Of course, I remember you."

You: "I didn't have many interactions with you at the time."

Them: "That's true."

You: "Would you be willing to visit with me for a few minutes? I've been out of school for two years working in retail sales, but I'm not happy with my situation. I'm not using my degree and I want get into advertising, but I don't know where to start. I remember you once said you'd help the agency's interns get into the business. Would you be willing to visit with me for 15 minutes? I'll work around your schedule and meet any time that's convenient for you."

Them: "Sure. I remember that, too. Let's meet Thursday afternoon at 3:30."

Not all cold calls end this way. But a lot of great stories begin this way.

Exactly What You Want Your Network to Do

Where does all of this relationship building and networking lead? Exactly how does this network help in the job search? What's the point?

It's actually pretty simple, but it takes some time. There are four things you want:

1. Someone to pass along a job lead, including the name of someone to contact inside the firm.

2. Someone to make a phone call for you so you don't have to write a cover letter… hence the title of this book.

3. A cup of coffee with a decision-maker in your network.

4. A personal introduction to a decision-maker.

After all the buildup to this section, those four things may seem short and anticlimactic. But they're not. They are all distilled trust. They require something from you. They require action from someone in your network.

14. **READ TWO PROFESSIONAL BOOKS EACH YEAR.**
Why: Increase your knowledge base in a rapidly shifting industry.

Something from You

Your past performance must be at a level that motivates someone to put their reputation on the line on your behalf. Which is OK. You're smart. You're coming out of an academic program that equips you to succeed.

Don't forget your performance also includes your significant background research on the firm where your network has contacts.

In the most challenging situation, you must convince someone that your future performance merits their taking a risk now. Your execution of the steps outlined earlier in the book should contribute to the likelihood they'll do this for you.

Something from Your Network

You are asking someone to add another task to their day. So don't be surprised if your request migrates to the bottom of their to-do list. Don't get discouraged. Just apply diplomatic frequency.

Very often, you'll need to do some reminding and nudging to move your network person into action. This skill is required in the business, too, so treat this as an opportunity to practice something that will prove very valuable in the near future.

Finally, understand you are leveraging someone else's confidence in you. This means you will ultimately repay that conviction with remarkable performance.

How to Ask

Here are examples of what an "ask" might sound like from you:

• Visit with someone who recently relocated from New York.

> "I'm moving to New York in two weeks. I don't have a job lined up, but I'm committed to finding a job where the major agencies are headquartered. Can you give me some suggestions?"

• Talk with a guest speaker who showed an interest in your career plans after their presentation to a public relations class you're enrolled in.

> "Have you heard of any job openings that might be a good fit with my goals and objectives?"

• Request a referral from an employee of an agency you're interested in.

> "Would you mind giving me a contact name inside the Hood & Wink Agency?"

• Close an "information only" interview after receiving very positive feedback on your resumé.

> "My plan of attack for finding a job is focused. We agree that my resumé includes concrete achievements and specific industry experience. You've seen the background research I've done on both the ABC Agency and their accounts. Would you mind calling one of your contacts in Account Services and introducing them to me by phone? I'll take it from there. All I need is an opportunity to demonstrate my skills and passion to get into the business."

• React to an instructor's offer to put you in touch with someone they know in the business.

> "Could we schedule a breakfast meeting with Kathleen? I'll work around both of your schedules and do the scheduling and coordinating. If you get the ball rolling with an e-mail to her, I'll make the call and set up the meeting."

• End an interesting but unproductive interview after your decision-maker gives you a contact at another firm.

> "Thanks for Steve's name. Is there anyone else you can think of who I should contact? Of course, I'll ask Steve if he knows anyone else I should talk to, but it would be great to have two or three other names from you. That way, I can have multiple leads in the works and increase my chances of hearing about job openings in other agencies."

• Conclude a conversation with the Chair of your academic department.

> "Would you mind making a phone call to one of the people you've mentioned today? I'd really appreciate it. I'll follow up promptly and say hello for you!"

• Review Your Plan with someone who worked at one of your Top 5 Agencies three years ago.

"90% OF ALL NEW BUSINESS IS WON AFTER THE THIRD SALES CALL ON A PROSPECT.

90% OF ALL SALES PEOPLE NEVER MAKE THAT THIRD CALL."

– EMORY THOMPSON
One of the world's best commercial tire salesmen

"All of my background research tells me to make a run at an Assistant Media Planner position with Carson & Company. Carson just made the final cut in the Subaru account review and you mentioned you knew a couple of media planners there. Do you feel comfortable referring me to one of those planners?"

• Learn someone in your network once worked on the client-side in San Francisco.

"I have a friend in San Francisco who has agreed to let me crash on his couch while I hunt for a job. I've stashed away enough money to last three months without a job, if that's what it takes. And my summer experience working nights in bank operations will allow me to work and look at the same time. Do you know anyone working in the Bay Area?"

• Hit a brick wall.

"I understand if you're not ready to refer me along right now. But if you'll tell me what I can do to get to that point, I'll do it. I've spent the last year working in a position that doesn't let me use my degree, and I'm ready to do whatever it takes to break into the advertising business. Will you help me do that?"

Just Ask

Ask for help. It's common practice. As everyone gives and takes a little, their networks form, reshape and break.

So don't let your pride get in the way. Don't think it's a sign of weakness to ask for a favor. It's not.

Likewise, don't underestimate the power of getting a lead on just one interview. An interview is where you demonstrate your desire and determination to break into the business.

It's also how you extend your network. Because at the end of every interview, you'll always ask the person you just interviewed with if they can think of anyone else to talk to.

All you need is one more person to talk to. That's not too much to ask.

It's how you get started in the business.

Sometimes It Goes Like This

From time to time, phone conversations with decision-makers looking for talented graduates go something like this. When they do, it's a great day.

Monday Morning

"Gene, I've been selected to start up a new agency to service one of our biggest clients. It'll be a small shop of eight to 12 people, but we'll handle the complete repositioning of a national retail giant. I need to hire the best student coming out of the department."

"That's great!"

"I want to interview three candidates and they have to be the best."

"Understood."

"I don't even have time to post the job. I need to talk to them this week. I'm packing up our house, but working in Texas all week. This thing is moving fast. The client wants the agency up and running in a month. I've already scouted out space and the interior design is underway. It'll be great."

"Sweet."

"Can you help me?"

"Sure. You'll have three candidates in your temporary office by mid-week. Give me your new cell number."

Sunday Night

"Wow! They're all three great candidates. Everyone came prepared with backgrounders on our parent agency and the client. One kid even brought in a plans book he'd pitched in his Campaigns class. The other two were as polished and poised as any of our junior AEs in the San Francisco office."

"Well, you said you wanted the best. I just gave them your name and number. And a little nudge, of course."

"But wait. They're all equal in presentation skills. They all pointed out key experiences at internships. All three asked for the job and said they're ready to start tomorrow. My CD and VP of Account Services coming with me to start the agency liked all three."

"I told you, these are the pick of the litter."

"Which one do we hire?"

"That's your problem. I've done my part. You can't make a bad decision."

Wednesday Afternoon

"Gene, Julie just accepted the position. She starts next Monday."

"She'll hit home runs for you."

She did.

Yes, dance.

This dance has to do with job hunting as it relates to the Top 10 Questions interviewers ask in interviews. It's a dance they were doing in 1983, and one your interviewer continues to keep busting out on the dance floor.

Once again, it's time to turn things upside down. Remember, this book asks you to take a different approach to finding a job.

What you need most right now is a way to add a measure of control into the situation.

Here's how to get it.

The Dance

To begin, you might ask, "What's wrong with the Top 10 Questions asked in interviews?"

Well, there are two things:

1. You still believe the Top 10 Questions exist for a good reason. Every job search site, every other "How to" book, every resumé writing seminar, every career counseling service and every HR department say these Top 10 Questions are important. Your class-mates and contemporaries who also are hunting for jobs pass them along.

2. You cling to the hope that your answers to these Top 10 Questions play an important part in getting a job.

You're wrong on both counts. "Why" will unfold over the next few paragraphs.

View the Dance through the Right Lens

Canned, published, accepted and repeated Top 10 Questions exist because interviewing potential employees isn't a regular part of anyone's job. More precisely, it isn't a daily part of the job for the manager who's making the final decision on the position for which you're applying. For your interviewer, this is a sporadic task that generally takes place when the wheels have fallen off the wagon, requiring everyone to take up the slack for the departing person.

No manager likes to conduct job interviews. No manager is fully trained and current in interviewing techniques. Job interviews always happen at the wrong time. They displace other, more fun tasks and consume precious time.

So every manager falls back on the classic "Top 10 Questions." As a matter of fact, these managers fall back on the same questions perpetuated by the 40-year-old business school rhetoric that no one believed when it was introduced in the 1960s. Such is the nature of business.

Why the "Top 10 Questions"? There are several reasons. They're easy to grab. They're all over the Internet. They're the questions the manager had to answer when he got hired. They're comfortable. Other managers ask the same questions. HR certainly won't be upset if the manager sticks with the Top 10 Questions.

What's not to like? It's a managerial no-brainer. Ask the Top 10 Questions and you're in safe territory.

Your Answers Don't Matter
Since the questions are rote, your answers fall into the same category. You don't really think your interviewer didn't also read the answers to the Top 10 Questions provided by every job search site, "How to" book, resumé writing seminar, career counseling service and HR department, do you?

That's how an author sells books to both job hunters and the people doing the hiring. That's how an author doubles their market.

The questions are expected. The answers are expected. It's the dance.

What to Do?
Create a new dance. Create a better dance.

Your New Dance
First, find a list of the Top 10 Questions.

"How can you say that after delivering the previous one-two punch?"

For one thing, your dance partner isn't on board. They've certainly never read this book. They expect you to have the same moves everyone else has. So this will take some clever maneuvering.

Keep reading.

First Steps

Since these Top 10 Questions generally are held in low regard and are of little use, they won't be repeated here. Go online and find them.

Enter the phrase, "Top 10 Interview Questions" into any major search site and you'll receive 2,050,000 results. Really... 2,050,000 results.

As a matter of fact, this may be the highest and best use of online job-hunting sites. They're easily accessible. You know every manager in a hurry will go to the same brand-name job-hunting sites as you do. Then they'll search for, find, print out and use the Top 10 Questions conveniently provided.

Keep that thought in mind.

Next Step, the Twist

Answer the Top 10 Questions – but with a twist.

As you answer the Top 10 Questions, your objective is not to come up with killer replies. Let me repeat that. Your objective is not to come up with clever, insightful, knowing, new, intriguing, fun and generally interesting replies.

Your objective is to have a practiced, relaxed, smooth, short, non-standard reply.

"Is that all?"

Yes.

"Why?"

Because what you want and, coincidentally, what your interviewer really wants, is to move the interview away from the Top 10

Questions hellhole. You both want to move the conversation toward some other, more interesting topic. In your case, however, you have a clear destination in mind.

Lead, Don't Follow
You want to lead this dance, not follow.

You want to move the interview away from rote questions, followed by rote answers. That dance isn't motivating to you, nor is it motivating to the manager who wants to get to the bottom of a few more important questions.

> "Are you smart?"

> "Do you work well in small teams?"

> "Will the team like you?"

> "Are you all show and no go?"

(Then, most importantly...)

> "How quickly can I let you work directly with a good client?"

To get there, you need to rapidly divert the conversation away from the Top 10 Questions.

Here's how to do that.

Answer the Top 10 Questions
Jot down 10 short answers. Don't spend a week formulating each answer.

Do spend a week on the transitions that change the conversation from one of your short answers to a question you want to get on the table.

Do review the connecting lines between Katiescope High Magnification and Katiescope Low Magnification discussed earlier.

Do review your Greg Audit.

This is where those things begin to come into play.

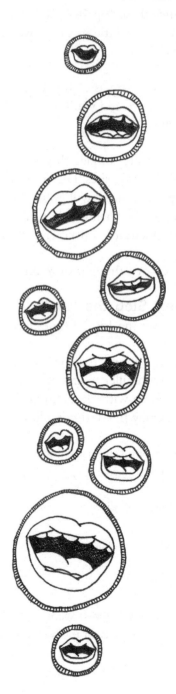

For Example

A Top 10 Questions answer, coupled with a devious conversation transition, might sound something like the following:

Interviewer: "What is your biggest weakness?"

You-to-yourself: ("I can't believe he just asked me that.")

Your Answer: "In tight deadline situations, I tend to take charge and run roughshod over people who can't make decisions. I do this to keep things moving along and not get jammed up at key milestones. On my resumé (you point to the paragraph with your finger and tap on it), you might have noticed the annual fundraising event I managed as VP-Social for the Texas Advertising Group. We drew over 160 members, but I had to push the VP-Speakers and VP-Finance to get their part done four weeks before the event. That took a little arm-twisting and some heated phone calls, but it worked. That's my weakness.

"I noticed on the agency's web site that you partner with the Crank Mullighan Foundation every year to pull off a similar event. Could we spend a few minutes talking about how your graphics and production teams work on that event? I'll bet it's fun! Do you...?"

What Just Happened?

Take a look at what just happened within your answer, which contains 10 sentences and runs about 30 seconds when delivered with a little energy and zip.

• Blunt Answer — The first two sentences directly answer the Top 10 Question with a quick "what and why." Incidentally, although these two sound like weaknesses when spoken, they *aren't* weaknesses from a managerial perspective. Thank you Katiescope and Greg Audit.

"In tight deadline situations, I tend to take charge and run roughshod over people who can't make decisions. I do that to keep things moving along and not get jammed up at key milestones."

• Grabber Detour — The third sentence literally highlights a vivid, relevant, illustrative accomplishment on your resumé. Your resumé is filled with vivid, active, relevant accomplishments, right?

"On my resumé (you point to the paragraph with your finger and tap on it), you might have noticed the annual fundraising event I managed as VP-Social for the Texas Advertising Group."

• Stand and Deliver — The fourth and fifth sentences crystallize and make vivid your "weakness."

"We drew over 160 members, but I had to push the VP-Speakers and VP-Finance to get their part done four weeks before the event. That took a little arm twisting and some heated phone calls, but it worked."

• Repeat Answer — The sixth sentence repeats the answer to remind the interviewer why we're here.

"That's my weakness."

• Redirect — The seventh, eighth and ninth sentences demonstrate that you read the agency's web site, noticed the print materials on the agency's "hall of fame" and did your homework before you walked in the door. They also move the conversation away from the Top 10 Questions — the dead end other candidates walk into.

"But, I noticed on the agency's web site that you partner with the Crank Mullighan Foundation every year to pull off a similar event. Could we spend a few minutes talking about how your graphics and production teams work on that event? I'll bet it's fun!"

• Go — Tenth, you end by focusing on the interviewer. You end here because you understand your job-hunting process is about them, not about you. You clearly communicate how you intend to make the interviewer get their job done more quickly, how you intend to accept responsibility and achieve goals, how you intend to help the interviewer win at their job.

"Do you…"

Rehearse

You must rehearse your answers to the Top 10 Questions. This is a little tougher than it sounds, but it's required. Even though you feel foolish doing it.

Personal interviews are nothing like writing. So practice in front of a friend. Your responses need to be aired and spoken out loud to smooth the edges. Rehearsals help you relax when you're responding to the interviewer, who's comfortably sitting in their office chair on home turf.

You might think you don't have the time to rehearse. You might think you can learn as you go. You might think you'll use the first few interviews to get this down pat. But what if you discover during one of those first interviews that this is the job you really want?

Rehearsals virtually guarantee you'll hit home runs in every interview. Most importantly, you'll score points by moving the conversation away from one of the more dreadful parts of job interviews.

One More Thing

If you're really smart, and you're approaching the end of a great interview with the impression that your interviewer also is very smart, go one step further.

Tell the interviewer exactly what you're doing and why you're doing it.

Tell them you really want this job. Spell out your preparation for the interview. Describe what you've gleaned as the key characteristics and skills the interviewer is looking for. Match those to your Greg Audit. Then tell them exactly what you did in the interview to move things away from a traditional interview format and toward what you wanted to talk about. In short, tell them what you just did.

The ability to articulate the strategy and spell out Your Plan is a terrific account management skill to have under your belt. It's a prized skill. It's worth pointing out to the person you're interviewing with if, and only if, that person happens to be a confident, skilled manager.

Spelling out this skill to a weak, vacillating, unfocused, self-centered interviewer is casting pearls before swine. Don't do it. They'll perceive you as a smart ass know-it-all and be frightened by you. You, on the other hand, would probably be better suited as their replacement rather than their employee.

How's that for attitude?

This chapter will only make sense if you paid attention in the prior chapter.

This is where you exercise control. Where you demonstrate your command of the business. Where you enable yourself to set the agenda in what seems to be an uncontrollable situation.

GEOGRAPHIC HIRE When an agency faces an immediate hiring need, they often interview and hire candidates who are on the ground. That is, interviewees who are attending (or graduated from) a nearby university. They might not even have a degree in public relations or advertising. But they already live nearby and walked through the door. So? They quickly can be trained in the agency's desired skill area, procedures and practices.

If you're interviewing in distant cities, you must overcome this disadvantage by traveling and interviewing at your own expense. Then you must convince your interviewer that you'll be in town and available to work on a specific date.

Or, you truly demonstrate your commitment to a particular market by moving there with no job offer in hand. This puts you into the geographic hire category.

Take the Offensive

You must push your way into advertising and public relations. You don't simply "present yourself" as someone ready and willing to work. That's not enough. That doesn't make sense. That's not what your interviewer is looking for in a recent graduate.

You must demonstrate your head is already in the persuasion business. In this case, you're in the business of persuading someone to hire you.

Advertising and public relations are not passive industries. To believe that the job-hunting process should be passive is nonsense.

So get ready to go on the offensive. When an opportunity presents itself, be prepared to strike. You want to have something to ask the person across the desk when they run out of inspiration, or are simply too tired to ask another Top 10 Question.

Create your own set of 10 questions to ask when someone says, "Do you have any questions?"

Have 10 Questions, Will Ask

Did you just notice the difficulty level has ratcheted up?

"Why is that?"

This is where creative thinking and concrete facts are coupled.

Observations you make during an interview join up with prior research. Unlike the Top 10 Questions discussed in the Dance chapter, Your 10 Questions concern things you are interested in. They center on your strong points. They ultimately illustrate something about you that is relevant to the interviewer. Or, they're simply fun.

Don't lose sight of a key fact, however: Your 10 Questions must deftly tell the interviewer about your applied research on the agency and its clients.

That is, Your 10 Questions are the product of your Katiescope Low Magnification. They tell the interviewer something about you. They are not just questions.

Your 10 Questions Are More Important than Answers

Haven't you been waiting years to encounter a situation where questions are more important than answers? Well, this is it.

These questions tend to sound something like the following:

"I went through the agency's web site last night and thought I had a pretty clear picture of your client roster. But I noticed some materials for Amy's Ice Cream on the wall in the conference room. Is that old exploratory work or recent work?"

"To get ready for today's interview, I've been reading The American Banker Online. I noticed there seems to be some editorial activity related to the current volatile real estate market. Is that the kind of issue that comes up in your management of the BanxBank account?"

"Well actually, I do have a couple of questions. On our tour of the agency, I saw some rough mock-ups for what looked like a video game directed at teens. The 'flying books' visuals

17. **KNOW WHEN TO CUT YOUR LOSSES.**
Why: See #12. Know when to stop. This varies.

were aggressive. Is that something you're working on for your pro bono account, the Minnesota Education Foundation?"

Wait... There's a Catch

There is a catch, but it's a good catch. It's good because this is what sets you apart from everyone else interviewing for the position.

Every single one of Your 10 Questions needs to be incredibly easy to answer. That's right, incredibly easy to answer. Stone cold, don't-have-to-think-too-hard, easy to answer.

Did you notice the second word in the title of this chapter?

Easy

These questions must be easy to answer. You will design them that way.

"Why?"

You're not testing anyone about anything. This is not an exam. You've left those kinds of questions far, far behind you. That's your old world.

In your new world, you're using questions to persuade the interviewer to hire you. You certainly don't want to put that person on the spot. You don't want them to stumble over the answer. You don't want them to think very hard. They're under enough stress already. They need something to help move things along to a conclusion.

So lob them a question that does that and more. Keep two things in mind when formulating your questions:

1. All of Your 10 Questions should comfortably (Diplomatically) move (Divert) the conversation to a topic that highlights your skills and interests (Devious). You want to get the interview pointed in a direction in which your follow-up questions flow easily and naturally.

This is where your applied background research again pays off. That's why you crafted Your 10 Questions using your Katiescope Low Magnification research.

2. Your questions make the interviewer look smart, feel good and enjoy the exchange. You'll be crafting these questions on the fly, so think fast.

18. **SAVOR SUCCESSES;**
NEVER FORGET LOSSES.
Why: The good and the bad; learn and remember.

Reread the Examples

They all start with a recap of something important about you: Your applied research skills plus your observation skills. Your understanding of the agency's client and their trade publication. Your insights on a competitor's recent move.

They are all easy to answer. Your interviewer will feel smart.

One Final Twist

Your 10 Questions all give you topics to research after the interview. That's right — after the interview. They give you something substantive to say to the interviewer the next day in your follow-up communication beyond "Thank You."

Is this new job-hunting process beginning to work for you? Remember to be:

- Diplomatic (Proactively take control of the interview agenda.)
- Devious (In a good way. It relieves the interviewer of a dull agenda.)
- Diverting (Switch to something substantive that relates to your interests and the interviewer's future success.)

TRAVELING ON YOUR OWN DIME INDICATES YOUR LEVEL OF COMMITMENT
Be prepared to go the extra mile. Or 200 miles. Or 1,200 miles. Block out two to four days in each city for interviewing. Call ahead and set up interviews with confidence in your voice. Target having two interviews your first day. Allow yourself enough time to get from interview to interview with time to spare. Once you're into the interviewing rhythm, you can add "opportunistic interviews" on top of your scheduled interviews.

What follows are nuts and bolts business concepts, intermingled with generally accepted advertising and public relations practices.

You're supposed to have picked these things up in school, during your internships and summer jobs, or through divination.

This somewhat lengthy section contains both mission-critical salary terminology and the very pedestrian importance of having your own business card. The topics are interrelated so read through once to get a sense of the connections. Then return for specifics.

You need a surface understanding of these topics to avoid tipping off the interviewer that you're a complete rookie. A blank stare on one of these, and you'll leave the impression you still have too much stardust in your eyes. That is, you might not be ready to enter the business. Or, you'll require some hand holding in the beginning. In either case, you lose a few points.

Last but not least, understand the nature of these business practices will vary wildly depending upon the size and age of the agency or firm. Expect rigid, standardized language and processes in larger firms. Expect rough-and-tumble, threadbare, take-it-or-leave-it language and processes in smaller agencies, where the business is colored by the owner's temperament.

Key Phrases

You need a few standard business phrases to get you started in the mechanical part of an interview. The five listed below are examples of generally accepted, business-like and diplomatically correct phrases. They're included here to give you some breathing room during an interview, or as a way to break into a delicate topic. You'll pick up the local variations quickly enough, but these can get you started:

> "Could we talk for a moment about the general salary range for this position?"

"Can you describe the agency's performance review process for me?"

"If I'm able to perform as well as I think I can, is there any possibility of a salary review prior to the agency's normal one-year review?"

"Is there anything in particular I need to know about the agency's benefits package?"

"This is exciting. Thank you very much for the offer. Will I be receiving an offer letter in a day or so with the details? As you can tell, I'm very excited about the prospect of working here, but this is an important decision. I'd like to have a day or so to be able to discuss this with my father/mother/spouse who works for the IRS."

Background on Starting Salary

You're concerned about the topic of starting salaries, and your parents are asking questions about this, too. Your friends are reading, hearing and passing along all manner of wild information on this subject. Your classmates are interviewing and perhaps getting job offers in a range of different starting salaries. This subject is one of the most hammered on topics of every job search site, and periodically is reported in the general press under the heading of "Salary Survey." Everyone wants to know what you're going to make.

The topic is important to you, because you view salary as a score or a grade. The higher the score, the better. It's good to have that perspective, up to a point.

Here's the point.

Face Facts

Although this is one of the most important topics to you, it's one of the most pedestrian topics to an advertising agency or public relations firm.

Why? Because just as it is in Las Vegas, the house always wins.

Advertising agencies and public relations firms are both in the business service sector.

An agency has only one thing to sell, and that thing is talent.

19. **VISIT, PHONE, E-MAIL. YOU CAN'T OVER-COMMUNICATE TO CLIENTS.** Why: Frequency pays off.

This talent takes on the business form of billable hours, or someone's time spent working on behalf of a client doing something.

In the business service sector, personnel costs are typically a firm's single largest expense category.

Agencies are required by their fundamental business model to pay as little as possible for entry-level salaries. They can, so they do.

It's the Price of Admission

The allure of the agency business and its rich, stimulating work environment ensures a steady stream of new job applicants, which drives down entry-level salaries.

Given the high pressure and demanding nature of the business, there also is high attrition and high turnover.

The only business model that makes any sense is to create conditions that attract the best emerging talent, motivate this thundering herd of flash and fire to perform at very high levels on behalf of the agency's clients, then quickly replace one of the herd when that person jumps ship to dramatically increase their salary.

That's not the whole truth, but it's close enough for now.

With that as the backdrop, here are some general, selective observations. Your results may vary.

Salary Negotiation

Starting salaries generally are not negotiated. Starting salaries typically are dictated by local wage conditions, the geographic cost of living, the agency's brand-name equity (its prestige and desirability), and the persistent allure of the advertising and public relations industries.

Salaries tend to be market specific. Starting salaries are higher in New York than they are in Nashville.

No, there isn't a "Salary Survey" contained here. It varies by city and by the overall market conditions that dictate how aggressive businesses must be to remain competitive. Use any good Internet search site to gather that information.

Salary Range

The operative phrase you need right now is "salary range for the position." This range spans the low end and the high end of starting salaries for a specific job function. In some instances, the range is rigid and formalized. At other times and in other markets, this range is little more than the prevailing salary required to attract a suitable pool of applicants when a position opens up.

Everyone starts somewhere on the range. Well, that's not really true. This "Salary Range" section and the two major sections, Performance Review and Salary Review Period, are joined at the hip. But here are the essential points to get the discussion started and give you a sense of how things work.

What's Normal

If you agree to start at the low end of the salary range with a performance review after 90 days and a salary review on the first anniversary of your start date, HR gets a gold star.

If you push for and get a starting salary at the midpoint with a performance review after 90 days and a salary review on your first anniversary, HR gets a bronze star.

If you push for and get a starting salary at the top of the range with a performance review and a salary review in six months, HR gets their ass kicked. Because in six months, the agency has no cards to play other than "non-salary compensation" (cooler office space, more responsibility, fewer ugly accounts, praise and adoration from the creative director, etc.).

You Have to Eat

Your starting salary will generally be a tight living wage. You're expected to be nimble enough and ingenious enough to learn the local ropes. Fortunately, there are informal but common agency practices to help you stretch a little and live well on the cheap. Here's why.

To a certain degree, an agency is motivated to help you with informal channels because, quite simply, you can't live in a cheap and frightening neighborhood or eat peanut butter sandwiches every day and still perform well at work.

Advertising is hard enough. You don't need major life issues also pressing in on you.

You can look forward to the following:

20. **DON'T TAKE IT PERSONALLY.**
Why: It's only business.
No one will die.

• At the drop of a hat, agencies may throw employee parties with great food.
• A pool of potential roommates exists inside almost every agency.
• Expect some help in picking safe, oddball neighborhoods and learning the local transit system.
• Vendors often feed the agency's junior staff. "Let's do lunch" is a real occurrence.

Nonetheless, Darwinism is in full play. This is not a sorority or fraternity. If you want to be in the business, you have to pay your dues. Low starting salaries are part of a system that determines who stays and who drops out.

Exceptions

Each of the previous "Normal" examples is an oversimplification, but not by much. And, of course, there are hilarious exceptions:

• An agency's client wakes up to the fact that it's possible to measure the effectiveness of advertising on the Internet. This is something the client has lusted after for years (the measurement part, not the Internet). With enough heat coming from the client, the media director might decide to go outside the normal salary range and agree to early performance and salary reviews to quickly attract someone who understands what's going on with interactive advertising.

> "Screw the salary scale. We could jeopardize an account that's worth $76 million in billings if we don't respond. Get some candidates in and pay what it takes. Worst case, the breakage outside the normal starting salary is cheap insurance. Best case, the candidate will be a technical whiz, the client will be instantly happy and not go shopping for some whacked out, interactive media-buying firm we'll have to coordinate with. Get going. Get the word out. I want interviews going by next week. Any questions?"

• A candidate for a position in the Creative Department brings in a stellar portfolio plus class project work, materials from an internship and published work done as a volunteer for a local non-profit organization.

"Did you see her portfolio? We have junior ADs that aren't performing at that level. Get her in and let's talk. Call Kim, the CD who's leading the Bronco account. Book lunch at the Petroleum Club for three. Let's not miss this opportunity. This might be a good long-term play."

• A recent graduate applying for an account management position finishes the first round of interviews with flying colors.

"Excellent resumé. Internships at three good agencies. Pitched to a regional management team from Radio Shack® who agreed to judge his school's student campaign projects. Our whole team loves him. We know he interviewed well at DDB; I called Steve and he told me as much. Make an offer now. You're authorized to immediately go $3,000 over if you have to, but he's got to agree to start in two weeks. Don't drag this out. Then push him hard to produce."

Sounds great, doesn't it? Ooooooh. I like that. That could be me! Action. High stakes. Drama. "Fly her in." "Get going." "Wine and dine." "Make the offer." All of which add to the allure of the business.

Just remember, these are exceptions. They are one in a 100 when the agency might hire 22 people a year. The rest of us have to push our way in with hard work and persistence.

Performance Review

A performance review is simply a manager's formal review of an employee's performance against their written job description. Are you beginning to see the value of having read dozens and dozens of job descriptions?

A performance review can mean an "up or out" decision within a 90-day probation period. Typically, this 90-day window enables an agency to legally operate under different rules during the very early stages of employment. New hires can be terminated without significant, disruptive, time-consuming, official HR processes kicking in.

It's not always that brutal, but that description comes close. In effect, it's a two-way safety valve. It protects the agency from an obvious, early bad match between a new employee and the agency. It also provides a frank, honest, graceful and swift exit path for someone who gets into the business, then learns they are not cut out for it.

Salary Review Period

Another related operative phrase you need to know has to do with the agency's salary review period. This is a key phrase. It determines when you have the chance for an increase in salary.

Where you start on the range and how quickly you're reviewed for both performance and salary advancement should be a relatively comfortable, mechanical topic for both you and the interviewer.

Although the topic is comfortable, the tension in the equation isn't. It boils down to the following conflict.

The agency wants to pay a low entry wage and see if you can perform. Their job is to get peak performance by dangling non-salary compensation carrots and ever-so-slowly reward performance excellence. That's simply good business practice.

You want to start at least at mid-range, press for a quick performance review, hope for an accelerated salary review based on stellar performance, then go for a promotion six months ahead of the normal cycle. That's because you're confident in your ability to perform.

Employee Benefits

This subject seems to come up because your parents — who are in a legitimate position to worry about this topic — want to scare you one last time before you leave the nest. They also want you to say something business-like during the interview. They think talking about a firm's benefits package sounds professional and very adult. In their world, it probably is.

The truth is, you are still among the Immortals. As a general rule, your age group doesn't place a high burden on an agency's employee benefits system. As a group, you tend to work very hard for peanuts, then resign for a better position with another agency after two to five years.

If the agency does something exceptional in this area, they'll point it out as a selling feature or issue a backhanded compliment to their competitors to get the point across.

Job Descriptions

Job descriptions are important before, during and after an interview. This section backs up and affirms the Katiescope Low Magnification discussion. All of your applied background research on job descriptions comes into full play.

However, the following comments tack on the notion that a job description will be of critical importance to you in about a year when you're up for your performance and salary review.

Job descriptions set the boundaries within which you are expected to excel. They also increase the probability you are managed properly and allowed to perform at a high level in a specific role the agency deems valuable and necessary.

Read Yours

After landing the job, read your job description periodically. Then keep in mind a few things about the individual who will be writing your formal, written, annual job performance review.

At best, in about one year, your manager will read your job description just before your annual review. They will reference the description as they complete their written evaluation of the work you've performed during the prior 12 months, and score you on how well you performed those duties. All of which sounds good and fair.

In truth, that reading of your job description will be the first time your manager has read it since hiring you. This places an unstated, ongoing obligation on you to ensure a high correspondence between your job description and your daily activities. In the rush and excitement of trying to do your very best on your first job, these two things can drift apart. That's not good.

So, it's a mistake not to read your job description every month or so to fully understand how your day-to-day assignments and duties fit your job description. Time flies in advertising. If you allow your actual duties to deviate significantly from what's contained in your job description, you can wind up performing a different job than the one you were hired to do. This can cause a problem during your annual review.

The solution is to learn to manage upward and keep your job description and daily actions closely aligned. It also focuses your

21. **LEARN TO USE ALL KINDS OF EQUIPMENT.**

Why: Required to move the production process past a crisis.

attention on documenting your achievements, and noting any material changes in the scope and responsibility of your job.

Manage Upward

Begin to learn how to manage upward within the chain of command. Know it's your job, not your boss's job, to document and organize your accomplishments.

Think of it this way: This is persuasive communication, not a chronicle of events. It's critical to your success and it's an incredible opportunity to control your destiny. You get to build a compelling case that clearly illustrates your contributions to the agency's success and, not coincidently, your boss's success.

Do the Following

- Read your job description once a month.
- Understand if, when and why you're drifting away from your written job requirements.
- Document what you do.
- Periodically give your manager a written summary of your accomplishments.
- Summarize to yourself what you do on a weekly, then monthly basis.
- Demonstrate how your performance contributed to the agency's success.
- Push for short, periodic bursts of feedback versus saving things up until your annual review date.

Job Offers

"I got one. What do I do now?"

How you handle a job offer is pretty simple.

First, if someone verbally offers you a position during the interview process, you don't have to say "Yes" or "No" on the spot. The person will (legitimately, strategically) pressure you to say "Yes," because they want to finalize the deal and get on with other business. But you're under no obligation to make an immediate decision. Why? The answer relates to the second thing you need to know about job offers.

Second, no offer is real until it is in writing, signed by someone in the firm authorized to commit the agency to this category of obligation. And this is a significant obligation.

If it's not in writing and it's not signed, it's not real.

For your part, you can't make a fully informed decision about the job offer based on incomplete information. You don't have the start date, salary, job title, performance review period, salary review cycle or company benefits in writing. So you truly can't make a fully informed decision.

However, you do need a positive, upbeat, business-like response to a verbal offer. Your tone of voice and volume will help communicate your desires.

Here are a few stock phrases you can draw upon in a hot spot:

> "Wow. This is an important decision. I need to think about it and discuss it with my Mom, who's an attorney with the Justice Department. We always talk things over."

> "I'm very flattered and excited almost beyond words. I'd like a day or two to think it over and..."

> "Thank you! This is exactly what I've worked and hoped for. May I have a copy of the offer in writing to review when I'm not quite so out of breath?"

> "Excellent! Thank you very much. I need a couple of days to consider the offer. That will give you time to fax me the offer in writing, and give me time to begin putting other pending matters aside."

That last example leads into another key phrase and bit of advice: Never open your kimono.

Open Kimono Questions

An "open kimono" question is a question intended to get you to disclose something that is not legitimately, directly and immediately pertinent to the business discussion at hand.

For example, if someone broaches the topic of your interviews with other agencies by asking, "What other agencies are you talking to?," smile and say, "I have several discussions underway. But I've been asked to keep those matters confidential, much like I assume you wish to keep the nature and content of our discussions private." In essence, you tease, parry, then stab.

Be very polite, but maintain discretion. The nature of these "other matters" is none of their business. Let the person asking the open kimono question sweat a little. You're sweating, aren't you? Share the joy.

Stay in Control

The person hasn't earned the right to ask an open kimono question, so you're not required to answer. In fact, if you do answer, it reduces your power and gives the other person the upper hand.

Remember, this is about control. You are not obligated to open your kimono to anyone during the job-hunting process.

When you hear these questions, understand what's going on. This person is looking for an advantage over you. Or, they're relying on you not knowing the system very well to achieve what they want — a quick end to the difficult task of finding a quality person for a position.

Here are a few open kimono questions and some suggested quick replies when:

• You're nearing the end of an interview and the topic of starting salary comes up.

> Interviewer: "What starting salary did you have in mind?"
>
> You: "I'm hungry and ready to go to work, but I'd prefer to open the discussion of salary by fully understanding your agency's salary range for the position we're talking about. Could you give me an indication of how that works?"

• An interview turns to the topic of career advancement opportunities within the firm.

> Interviewer: "How soon do you think your review should take place?"
>
> You: "Since I'm from Texas and considering several positions in the Chicago area, my expectations may be a little out of range for this market. As you can tell from my resumé, my past performance has been promptly rewarded a number of times with promotions and a salary bonus once. What is the agency's typical review cycle in high-performance situations?"

• A decision-maker lets it be known that she's very well connected with all of the media directors in the market.

> Interviewer: "What starting salary has the Wink & Knodd Agency put on the table?"
>
> You: "My understanding with Wink is that their salary discussions with me remain confidential. But again, I'm very interested in working here. And I know you will be very competitive in the market, because you have a track record of attracting very talented people. That's one of the primary reasons I want to work here."

22. **TAKE A BREAK. GO AWAY.**
Why: Take no work. Make no calls. Everything is fine.

• The interview went great. Everyone is excited about your experience, accomplishments and interviewing skills. The manager you're interviewing with is ready to close the deal.

> Interviewer: "Well, do you accept? The offer is firm. You have my word on it."
>
> You: "I am flattered and excited. This is a very big decision, and I'm treating your offer in the most serious way I know. But I need a day or so to consider all of the various things we've talked about today."

• A hot manager in a hot agency puts you on the spot.

> Interviewer: "What would it take to get you to commit right now?"
>
> You: "That's an aggressive question worthy of an aggressive answer. If you'll prepare an offer letter right now spelling out everything we've talked about today, we can wrap up our discussion and I'll call you within 24 hours with a decision."

• At the end of the day, it's your call. Here's the ultimate, legitimate, bottom-line, perfectly acceptable, business response to any open kimono question you don't want to answer. You get to draw the line. It's your life. You are ultimately in control.

> You: "I'd prefer it that way, and that's reason enough."

Business Cards

Business cards are important. You need one. You also must get one from every decision-maker you speak with, because this allows you to ask for permission to stay in touch after the interview. It's a ritual every business person in the world knows. Keep it simple. Upon being introduced, you say, "I'm very pleased to meet you. Here's my business card. May I have yours?"

Yours
Your business card should contain your name, address, phone number and e-mail address.

Use Helvetica as the font with black ink on heavy, bone white business card stock. Avery.com, an established brand name in the envelope business, has downloadable software compatible with MS Word® that lets you create business cards using word processing software. And of course, Avery sells die-cut, sharp-edged prepared card stock sheets through almost every major office products retail store. This card stock works with Avery software to produce perfectly acceptable business cards for someone entering the business.

Graphic elements, fancy fonts, colored paper and irregular sizes and shapes draw attention away from your name, which is the most important item on your card.

A great story concerns the chairman of the board of one of the oldest, most prestigious automobile manufacturing firms in the world. His business card simply had his name with the word "Workman" printed underneath. This served as a reminder of his humble beginnings and as a continuing connection to the craftsmen who built the cars.

Theirs
Don't leave any interview without getting your interviewer's card.

Hand them your card and ask for theirs.

This ensures you won't misspell their name, get their title wrong or be caught without contact information.

Always Ask for Permission
As you accept their business card say, "Do you mind if I stay in touch?" They almost certainly will say, "Yes" or "Of course."

This is an absolutely critical step in Your Plan.

This gives you permission to follow up on your interview several times, in several different ways, which is one of the cornerstones of this book.

Plus, you need that card for motivation and as a concrete reminder of the person. Later in the day, note the date and time of the interview on the back of the card.

Audience Perspective

As you near the end of this book, you should reread Chapter 3 with a new perspective. Go ahead, it's only a few pages long. That rereading will solidify why the entire process described in this book works. As promised, what began in Chapter 3 ends here.

With respect to frequency in the context of Your Plan, the key is to directly benefit your interviewer and potentially help that person look good in their clients' eyes.

This is frequency with an audience perspective.

Applied Background Research Required

Your continuing applied research is relevant during your follow-up. Nothing else matters.

Thank You cards are effective, but send only one to each person. Sending more than one will be perceived as naïve.

Jettison the notion that frequency means a high volume of mail. Without relevant content, your frequency will instantly become junk mail. It will never be opened, much less read.

Discard the thought that your follow-up content is about what you've done. You're missing the point. The person you interviewed with doesn't care what you're up to or what personal/professional progress you've made since the interview. News about you is not relevant to them, means little and is, quite frankly, the height of egotism. This is hardly what you want to convey.

Let's Take a Closer Look

What Type of Frequency?
• The only kind of frequency that works is frequency with permission.

It's why you asked for their business card, then asked if you could stay in touch.

23. **KNOW A GOOD RESEARCH LIBRARIAN.**
Why: Experts at finding anything. Fast and uncanny.

• The only kind of frequency that works requires you to deliver relevant content.

The material is limitless. It might be a topic uncovered in one of Your Top 10 Questions, a product review, trade press news about the agency's client, industry perspectives by a sector analyst, a national magazine article or a local news article... the list goes on forever.

• The only kind of frequency that works is timely.

News items dim quickly, so timeliness is important. In fact, timeliness trumps uniqueness. The agency's research team already may have supplied the piece to your interviewer, but that's OK. By sending something newsworthy, you elevate the information and emphasize its importance. Your interviewer can pass along your copy to their client.

• The only kind of frequency that works is persistent.

Once a week, every other week, three times a month, it doesn't matter. As a matter of fact, if it's regular as clockwork, that might not be good. It might be perceived as becoming too routine and not tied to the ups and downs in the client's business.

The quality and tone of your applied research must be self-evident. But don't worry about that. It's everything else about your frequency that makes the difference.

THE MASTER OF FREQUENCY Jim McDonald, whose career spans both the agency and client sides, is one of the masters of frequency.

Traveling in a time well before today's airport security focus, Jim would do the following. Just before boarding a business flight, he would pick up *The Wall Street Journal*, *The Washington Post*, *The New York Times* and the daily newspaper from his clients' hometowns. At the start of each flight, his briefcase looked like a newspaper route man's.

Also tucked into that bulging briefcase was Jim's address book, a fistful of his agency's letterhead envelopes, a roll of stamps, a pad of yellow sticky notes and a pair of scissors.

On the flight, Jim would cut out articles, write notes, then hand address, stuff and stamp envelopes to his clients.

As he exited his flight, the newspapers went into a recycling bin, the somewhat smudged and bent letters went into the airport's public mailbox, and Jim washed his hands of newspaper ink at the first chance.

All of Jim's clients knew when he was traveling. They could tell by the condition of the envelopes. They also knew he was working for them while others slept or read books.

When Can Frequency Work?
- You can use frequency to capture a decision-maker's attention during your attempt to schedule an interview.
- You can use frequency to remind someone of your name after an interview.

Why Does This Type of Frequency Work?
- It benefits the recipient.
- It brings you up to speed so you're already running when a position opens up.
- It allows you to repeatedly say to the recipient, "If a job opens up and you need someone already prepped on the client, I'm ready."
- It reminds you of other career opportunities with competing agencies, the client-side and the media.

What Works?
- Articles torn out of publications
- Newspaper articles cut out and pieced together with tape
- "Print friendly" copies of online articles
- Posters, flyers and POP materials collected during ground-level, retail research
- FSI from local newspapers
- Articles from local niche newspapers too small for the agency research team to care about
- Direct mail pieces you receive
- Digital camera images of public happenings, outdoor boards or newsworthy events
- Collateral materials from trade shows

What Do I Do?
Deliver anything on the list above with a signed sticky note attached:

> "Thought you might not have seen this."

> "This relates to our discussion on Wilson Homes' new competitor."

> "An RFID article from Business Week!"

> "The key quote is highlighted in the fifth paragraph."

Sign your note. Use plain, printed stationery notes if your handwriting is so bad no one can read it.

What Else?

Keep a photocopy of what you send. This does three things:

1. The expense and bother of photocopying will force you to be selective in what you send and, coincidently, prevents you from falling into the trap of sending too much.

2. You automatically have something to take into your next interview with the person as a reminder of what you've been doing.

3. If you hit a dead end, you can use the same information with a competing agency or with the client.

Get to Work

Create a spreadsheet, print it out, blow it up to the largest size available on a local photocopier and thumbtack it to a wall. Scribble in dates, places and things you've sent. More importantly, don't forget to make note of feedback you receive from people in the form of phone calls, e-mail replies and passing remarks after follow-up interviews.

This achieves two things. First, it's motivating to see Your Plan take shape. Second, you'll quickly identify the agencies, people and sectors you are drawn to by the volume and nature of your notes. This keeps you focused, but also can be a signal to trim away unproductive leads or redirect your efforts to the client-side or a competing agency.

Your research needs to be current. Your delivery has to be timed properly. Your delivery executions need to vary. You must be incredibly persistent. An upbeat and positive attitude should be evident at all times. And... all of this must take place with little or no immediate response.

Remember: The burden is on you to break into the business. Organization, intelligence and persistence are requirements. Your execution of this follow-up plan is concrete evidence you are ready to be hired. The content of your messaging is ample evidence you'll be a quick start on an account, which is valuable to the agency.

You are demonstrating your command of the business during your job hunt.

Timing

There is no magic formula on how often to mail things, or when to call and schedule a follow-up interview. Use your own good judgment. Use the frequency of news surrounding the agency's clients or their industry. Use breaking news about a communications or technological development as a timely opportunity.

Consider something similar to what's outlined below as a follow-up to a Tuesday interview. These are delivery dates, not sending dates. You'll want to avoid having your communications arrive on Mondays when things are likely to be overlooked or put aside in the normal crush of the week's beginning.

Tuesday:	Interview
Wednesday:	Thank You note
Friday:	First news article
Tuesday next:	Second news article
Tuesday next:	Third news article
Tuesday next:	Schedule a follow-up interview; tell the person you're still interested; it's been three weeks.
Tuesday next:	Fourth news article

Continue, continue and continue… to demonstrate your incredible discipline and persistence.

24. **COST, QUALITY, QUICKNESS.**
Why: Pick two.

ASK FOR THE BUSINESS Mike Rawlings, former CEO of TracyLocke Advertising in Dallas, was the master at asking for the business when leading a new business pitch.

As soon as TracyLocke was named as a contender, and throughout the entire review process, he closed every phone conversation and personal interaction with some variation on the following question: "Why don't you go ahead and name TracyLocke as the agency of record right now?"

When asked by a potential client why he did this on every possible occasion, the reply was straightforward and simple. "TracyLocke is clearly qualified to handle your business. That's why you included us in the competitive roster. I'm simply giving you every opportunity to say 'Yes' before the formal presentations take place. If you do say 'Yes', it will be a solid business decision. You'll immediately have a great agency working on your account. It will save my agency a significant amount of new business pitch expense. Will you name TracyLocke as the agency of record right now?"

Ask for the business.

Ask for the Job

Periodically, intersperse the message that you're still in the job market, and obviously still interested in working for the person you're sending things to. Close the deal. Ask for the business. This is a key professional skill some people overlook.

Be blunt. Be honest. Be professional. It's part of the business. If you don't ask this critical question, they can't say "Yes."

Maintain Multiple Fronts

Right about now, the impact of selecting your Top 5 Agencies and each one's Big 3 Clients should be dawning on you.

You are not in the business of working for free. You are in the business of finding a job. With five agencies and a total of 15 clients in your applied research folder, you should have several initiatives underway.

Leverage Your Work

If you hit a wall, take the latter part of your communications stream and pursue things on the client-side of the equation, with a competing agency, with a trade organization or with the industry news media.

There's nothing unethical or underhanded about doing that. This is business. It's your sweat. Everything you're sending requires incredibly hard work to put together and it's taking place on your dime. So leverage your work.

Don't Stop

There also is no magic "End" button. Your timing may slow down to once or twice a month in some cases. Even so, as long as you're in the job hunt, keep some level of frequency going.

Why? Things change. People leave for other jobs. People up the ladder get promoted. Agencies win new clients. Companies expand. A market cycle will begin an upswing. Technology shifts require that someone with current knowledge be brought on board to address the change. That's why.

Bend

Get into the rhythm of asking your interviewer for names of people you also should contact. This is how you uncover additional leads. Follow up on the leads with quality work.

But remember, not every lead merits the benefit of your hard work and frequency. Think about the following: Your interviewers should earn their way into your job-hunting campaign. This prevents you from burning out or pursuing a job lead where the person doesn't give something back to you in recognition of your effort and desire to be in the business.

If that sounds like the beginning of a network, you're on to something.

PART III
The End

"That's it?"

Yes, that's it.

It might look as though it won't work, because it requires patience – and your heart is already pounding. It might sound difficult, because it involves "research" and you dreaded going to that course all semester. You think this kind of self-analysis is the stuff of self-help books. Or, you think mailing things to people is ineffective, and you'll fall into the same category as all those credit card offers you've received over the last six months.

Last but not least, you can't even imagine being as pushy, forward, persistent and assertive as this method proposes. You believe people will think you have a big head, that you're an egotistical smart ass and don't deserve to be in the business.

None of those things are true.

Why Does This Book's Job-Hunting Strategy Work?

Simple. It stays firmly focused on the interviewer's perspective, but uses that perspective to your advantage in five important ways:

1. (important) It encourages you to demonstrate the very traits and characteristics the person doing the interviewing is looking for — creativity, initiative, research skills, persistence, discipline and the smart use of frequent contact in an over-communicated world.

2. (very important) It directly benefits the person you're interviewing with — your work can potentially make them look good in their client's eyes.

3. (more important) You can leverage your background research several ways; that is, with another agency, with the client, with

one of the client's competitors, or with the media reporting on the news within the client's industry.

4. (most importantly) It gets you started in the business on your own, before you're hired. You're already running at speed when an opportunity presents itself to a decision-maker who needs to make a "quick hire."

5. (mission critical) It gives you a way to exercise some control over your job hunt, and not cede this control to a person who is overworked, stressed out and too tired to return your phone call.

BE HEARD As a general rule, you are too polite. Be assertive. It is almost impossible for you to go over the top. For your entire academic life, you've been on the receiving end of things. You're smart. You're a quick learner. You (politely) listen and learn. You are motivated. You are as prepared as anyone can be for entry into the business. But each of these excellent things is on the inside. No one can see them!

This is a new chapter. It's time to change.

Speak up. Learn to "grip and grin" — shake hands and smile — that's when you are most powerful. String a few sentences together. Ask some really good questions. Take control during parts of the conversation.

It's a conversation. It's a dialogue. It takes two to play.

Start playing.

This Is Your Beginning
This book is of no use if you don't execute on all levels. Nonetheless, there are some realities that should be addressed.

Worried Everyone Will Follow Your Plan?
Don't worry.

The process described in this book is incredibly hard work, in much the same manner the public relations and advertising business is incredibly hard work.

Its difficulty ensures that weak competitors will flail away at this method, then quickly fall away.

Adapt
Astute job hunters will modify this process, twist it to their own style and come up with a better way. Or, they will leave out, leap over and skip steps. Much in the same way advertising and public relations professionals do all the time.

Don't worry. You'll find your way. This book also can act as a springboard.

Focus

You must make the initial decisions to focus your attention and efforts:

- Pick a city.
- Select five agencies, or five clients or one of the media.
- Commit to a discipline: Account Management, Creative, Media, Public Relations, Production, Research, Administration, Operations, Sales or a Specialty Area.

Your choices don't close future doors. They open the industry door, which then allows you to see an almost unimaginable array of other fun doors to explore.

Katiescope and Greg Audit

Do you really have to do all of that for Your Plan to succeed?

In a word, "No." Do as much as you can, then stick with the process at a level you can sustain. Don't bite off too much or you'll choke.

But do run the numbers.

Half of your competition for a job won't even attempt to do any background research. It's too hard. They believe they left research behind when they walked across the stage and were handed their diploma. Or, they're just too tired to try. You know who these folks are. You've been in group projects with them. They're the ones who left early.

Of the remaining half, a few will attempt the process outlined in this book, but will get distracted or not truly understand the required audience point of view. They wind up shooting themselves in the foot. You know who these folks are. You've seen them hopping around on one foot.

Of the small fraction left, some will accept a position with other firms, some will abandon their efforts and follow a significant other to another city, and some will panic early in the hunt and switch to online job hunting.

That leaves you standing almost alone: Ready to use applied

background research to narrow your focus, willing to let your research distinguish you in an interview and able to continue the hard work required to keep your name top-of-mind when a manager suddenly has a position to fill. Frequency works in advertising media, and the right kind also will work for you in your job hunt.

That's all you have to do.

Expect Success

Do It
Successful people do what unsuccessful people don't do. It's not that unsuccessful people can't, or won't, or don't know how, or aren't able to or don't have the opportunity. They just don't.

What are you waiting on?

And Then Toss This Book
The purpose of this book is to help you succeed in finding a job in advertising and public relations. The true measure of success comes when it's tossed aside.

Soon.

As you get going, lay this aside and let your job-hunting process evolve. You no longer need this book. As a matter of fact, you don't need me or anyone else telling you what to do.

You're in the business.

Congratulations.

One Day, Return the Favor
Take the phone call from a somewhat intimidated college student facing graduation.

Answer the e-mail that begins with, "Gene suggested I contact you...."

Have coffee with them, even though it adds an hour to a very long day.

Because you remember.

25. **APOLOGIZE ONCE AFTER MISTAKES.**
Why: Clients only care about what you're doing about it right now.

Index

CPSIA information can be obtained
at www.ICGtesting.com
Printed in the USA
LVOW03s0352140117
520832LV00020B/35/P